The Coloring Studio

Extraordinary Machines

Claire de Moulor

LB
Little, Brown and Company
New York Boston

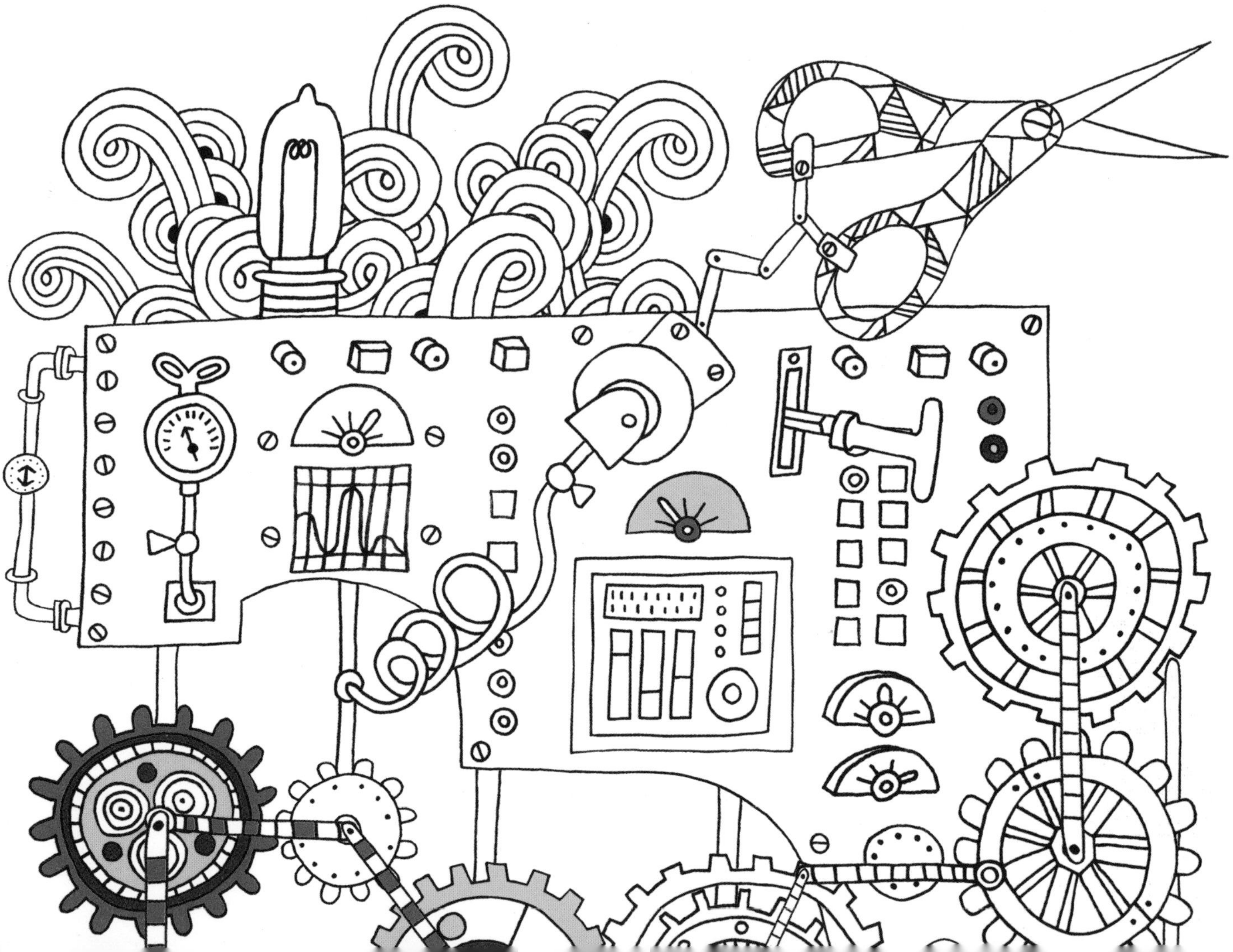

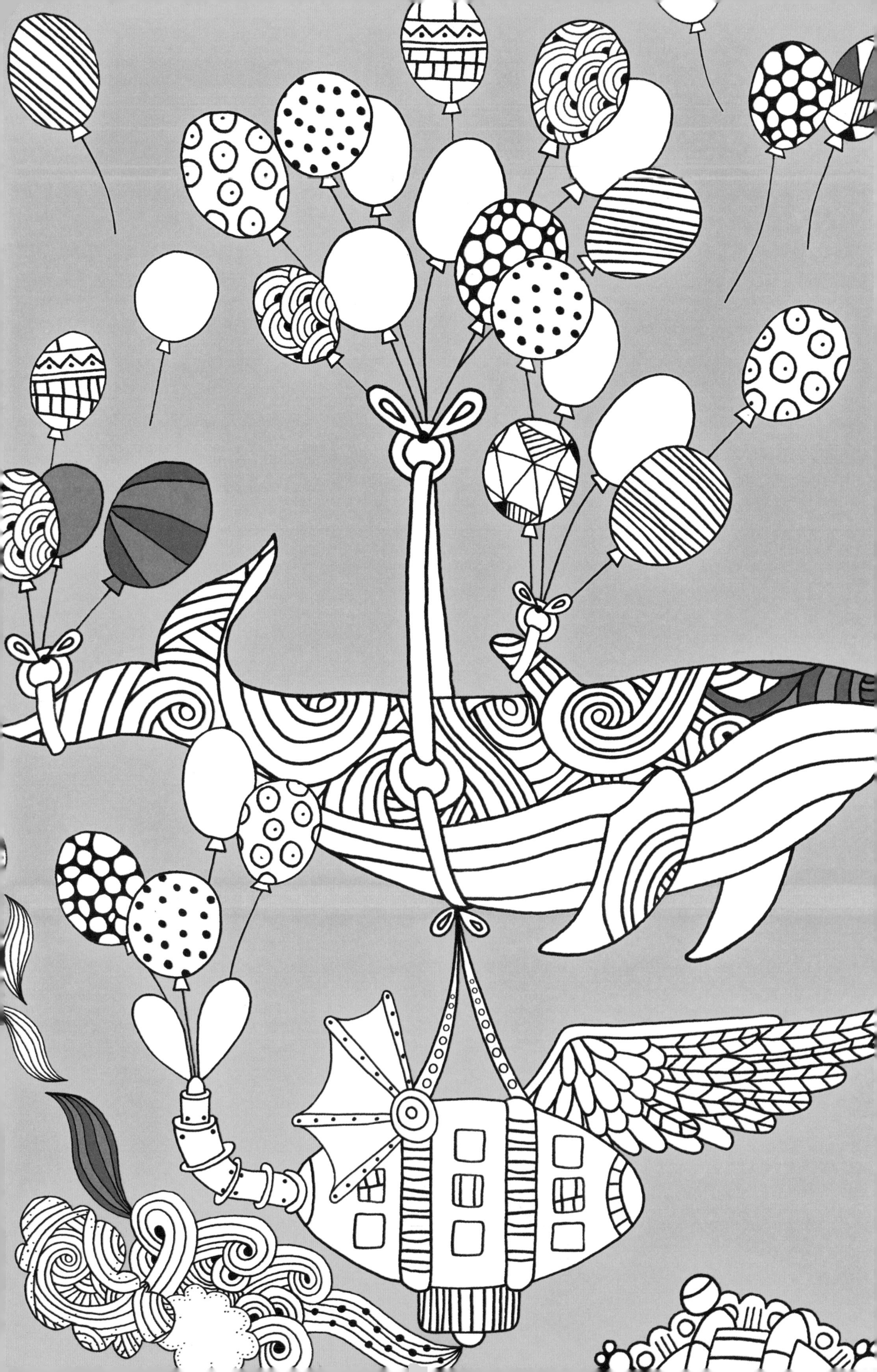

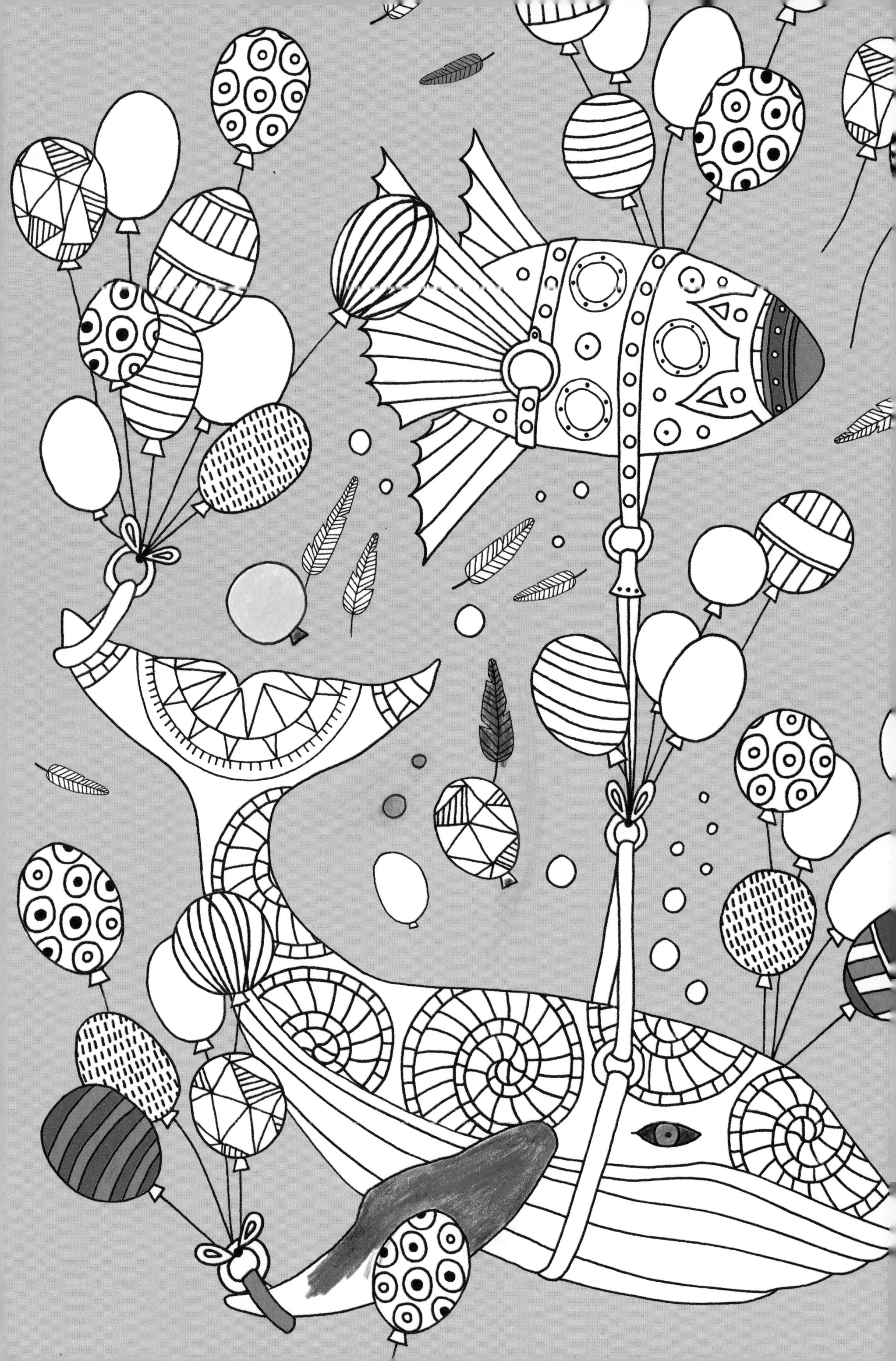

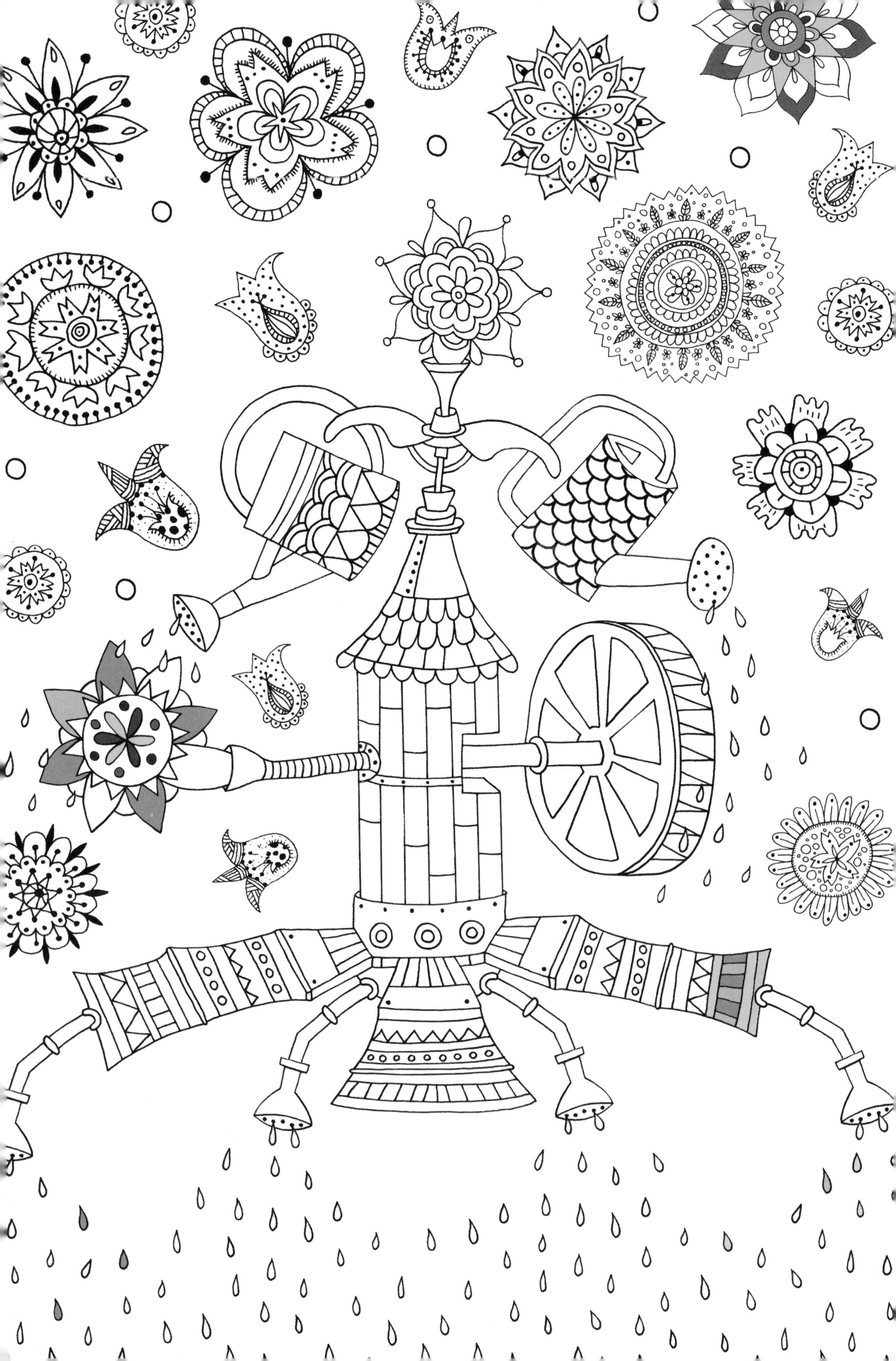

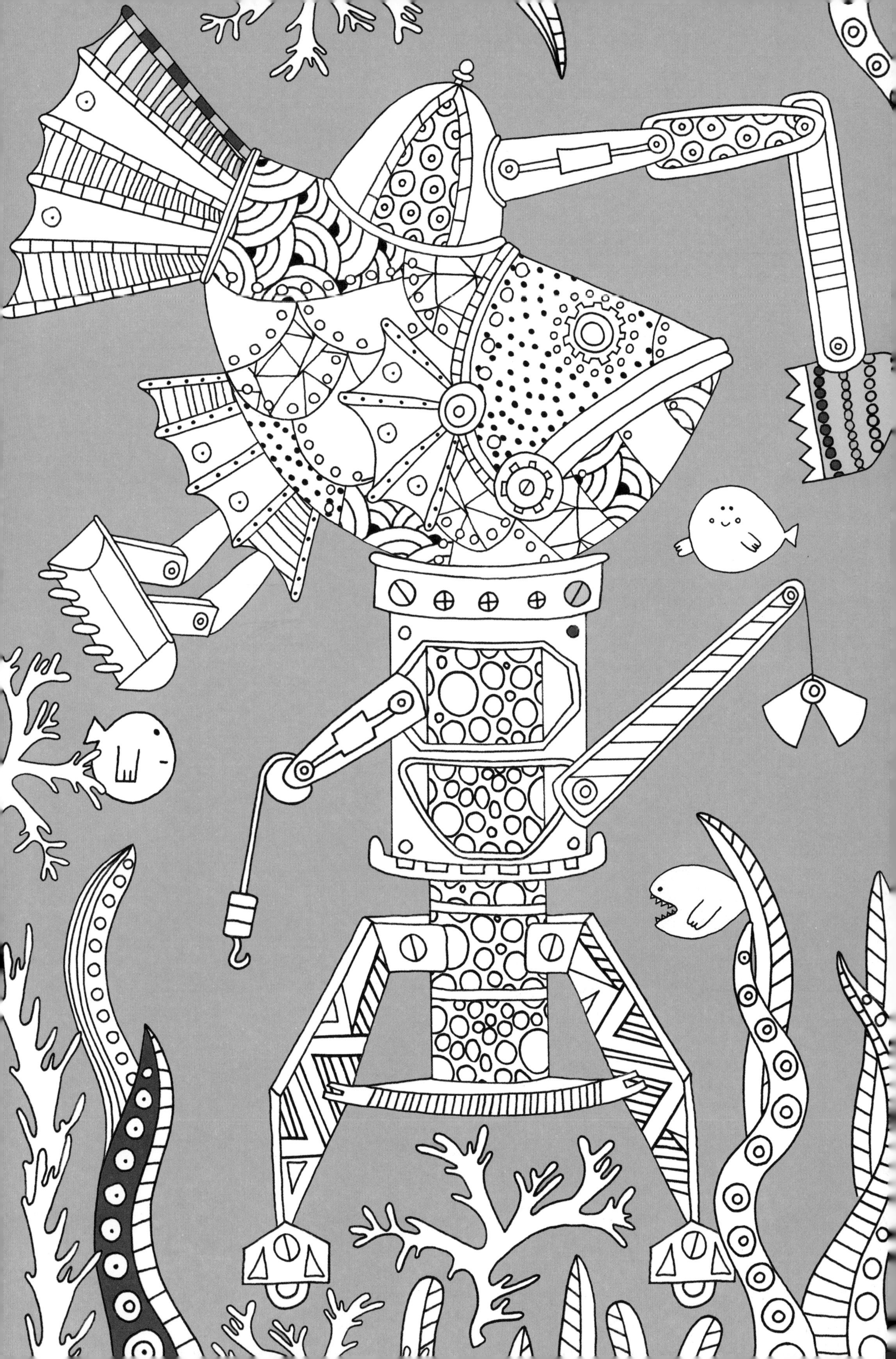

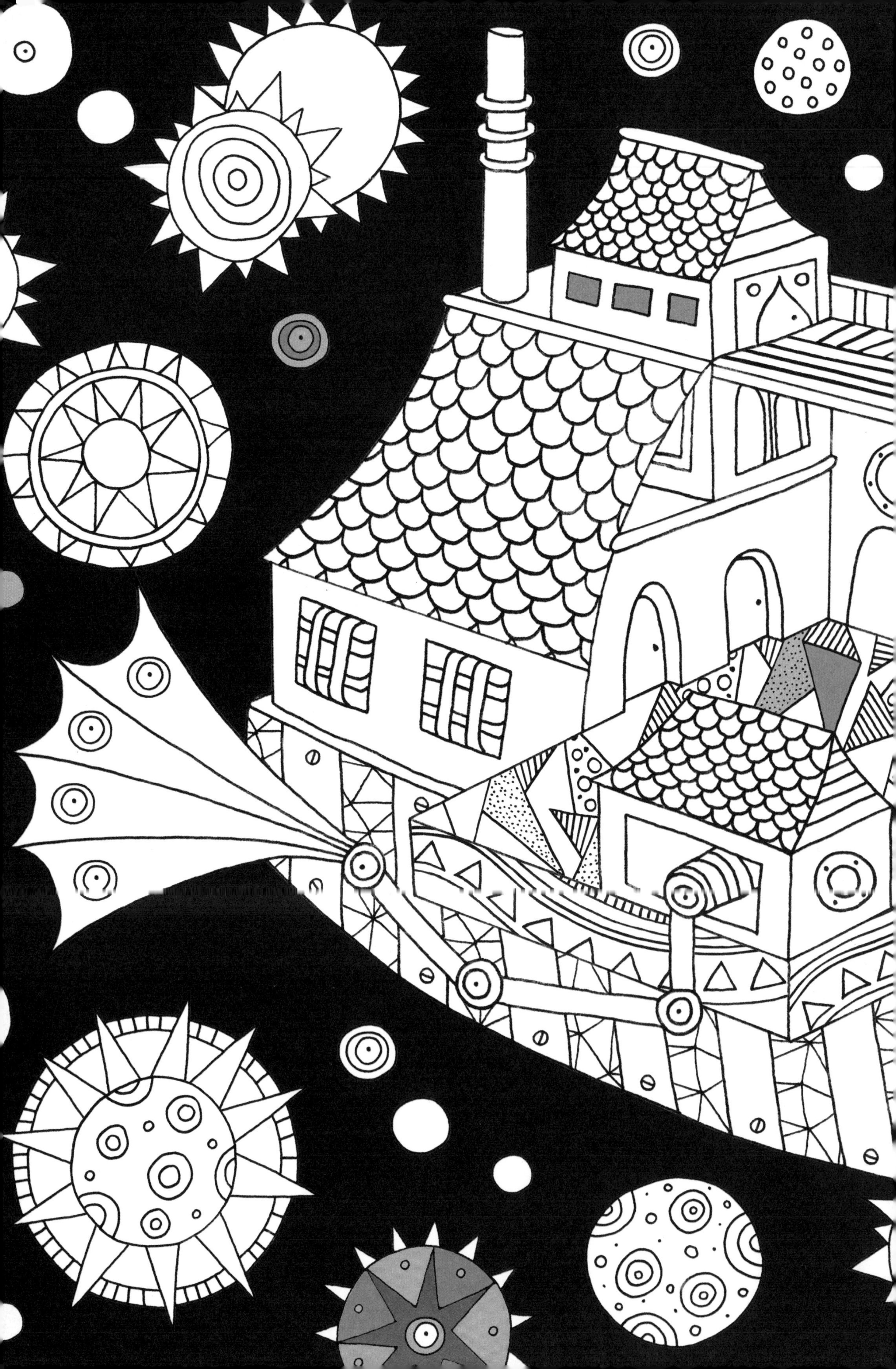

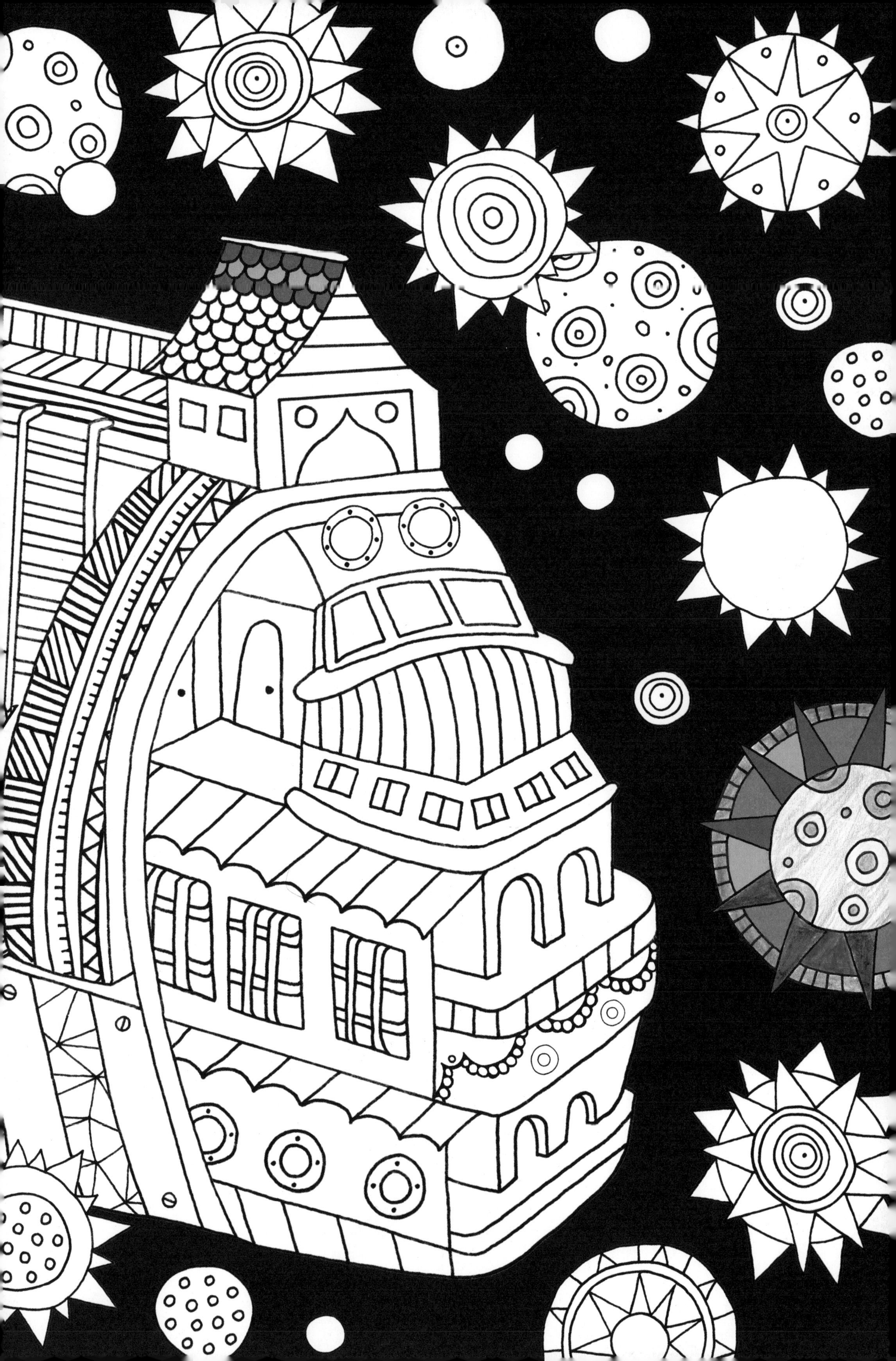

N

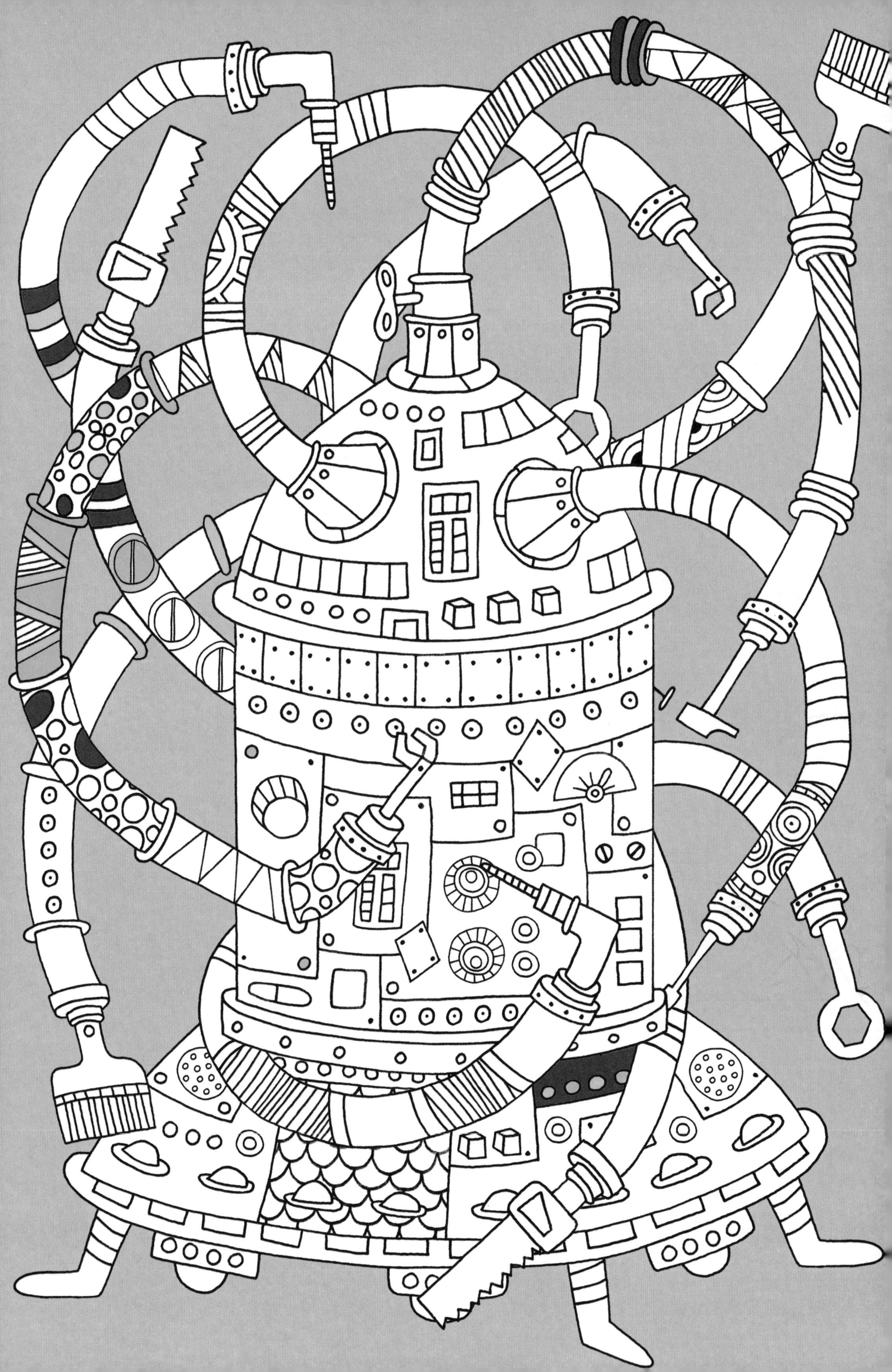

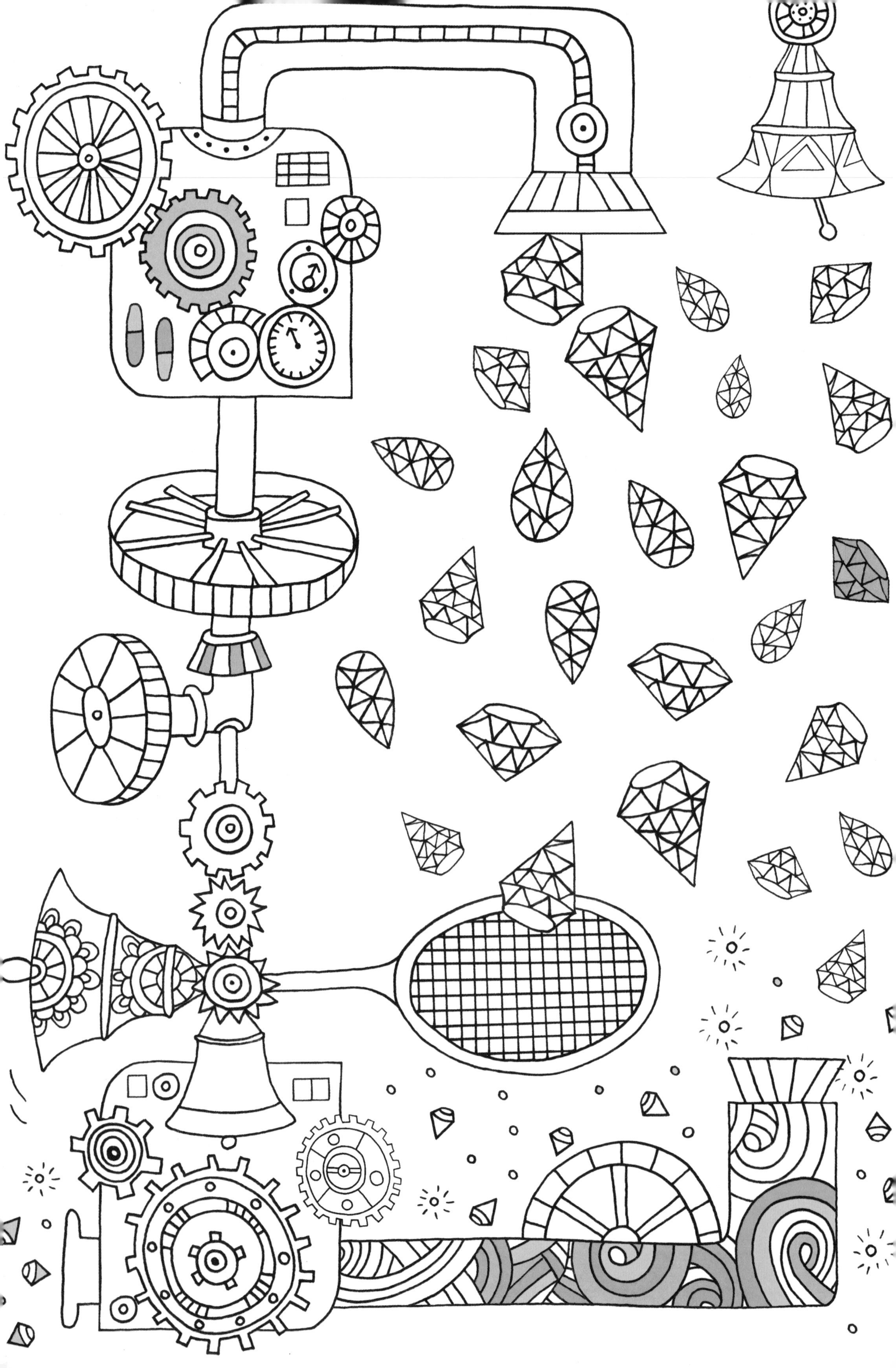

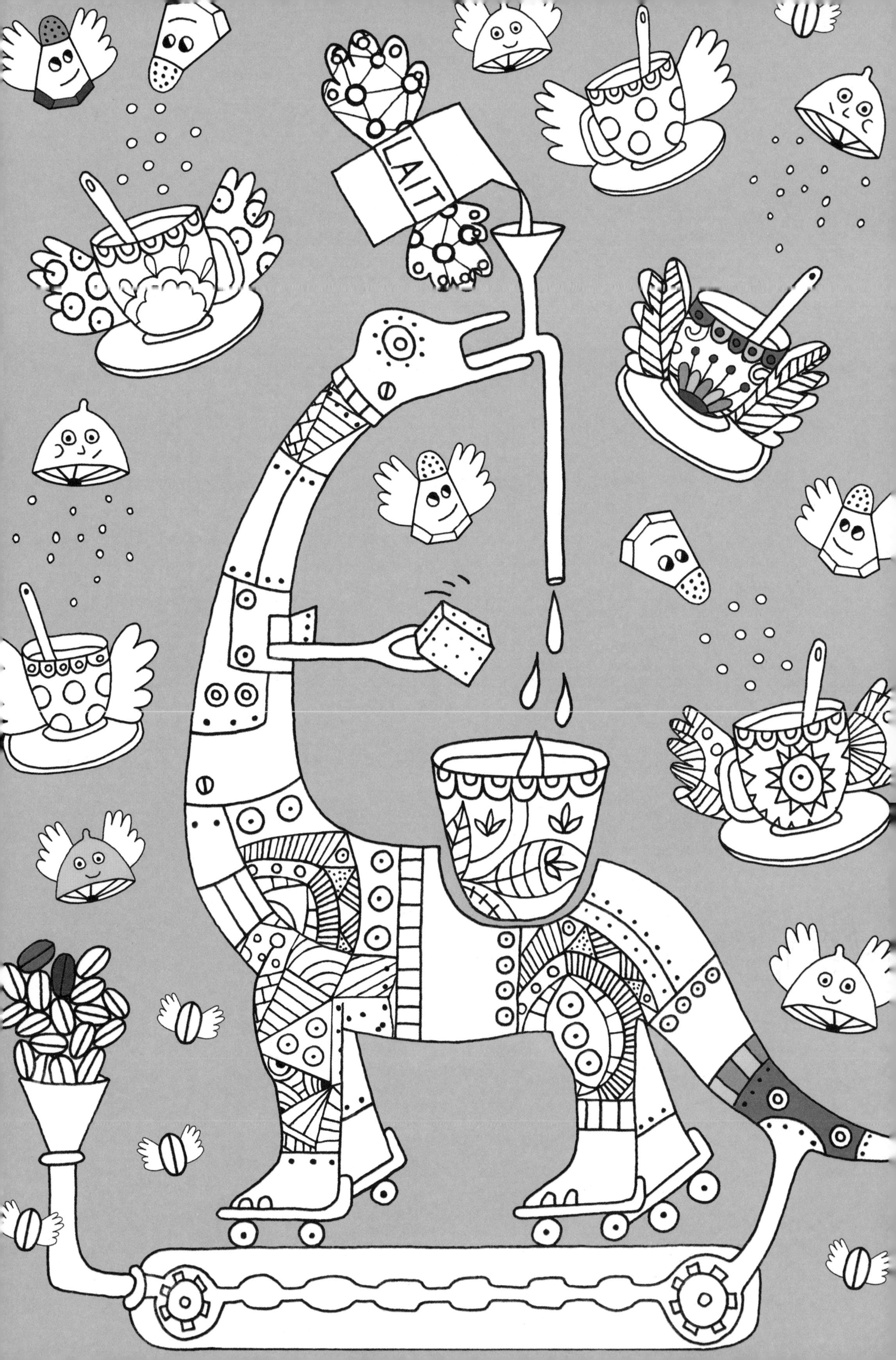
LAIT

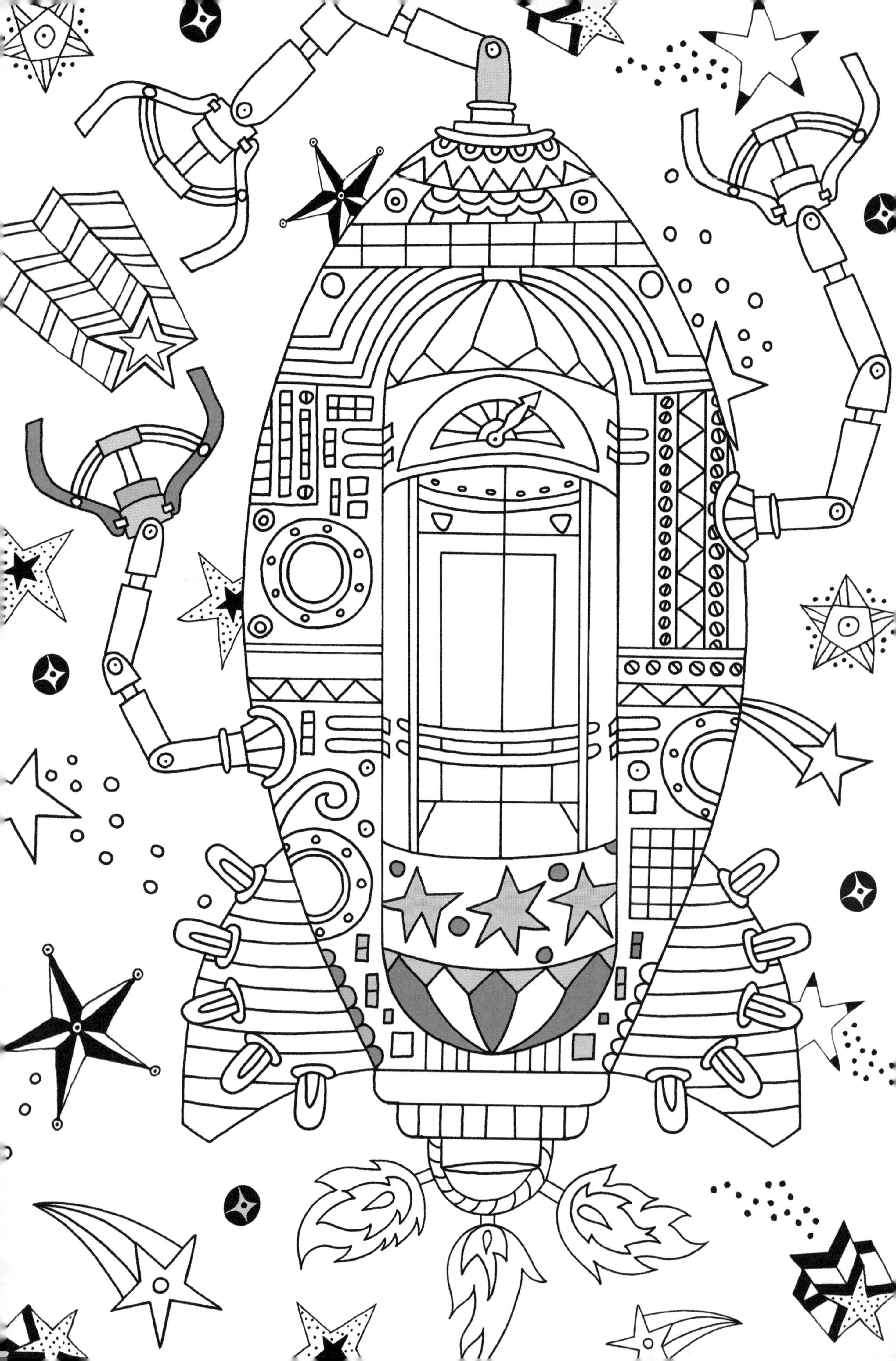

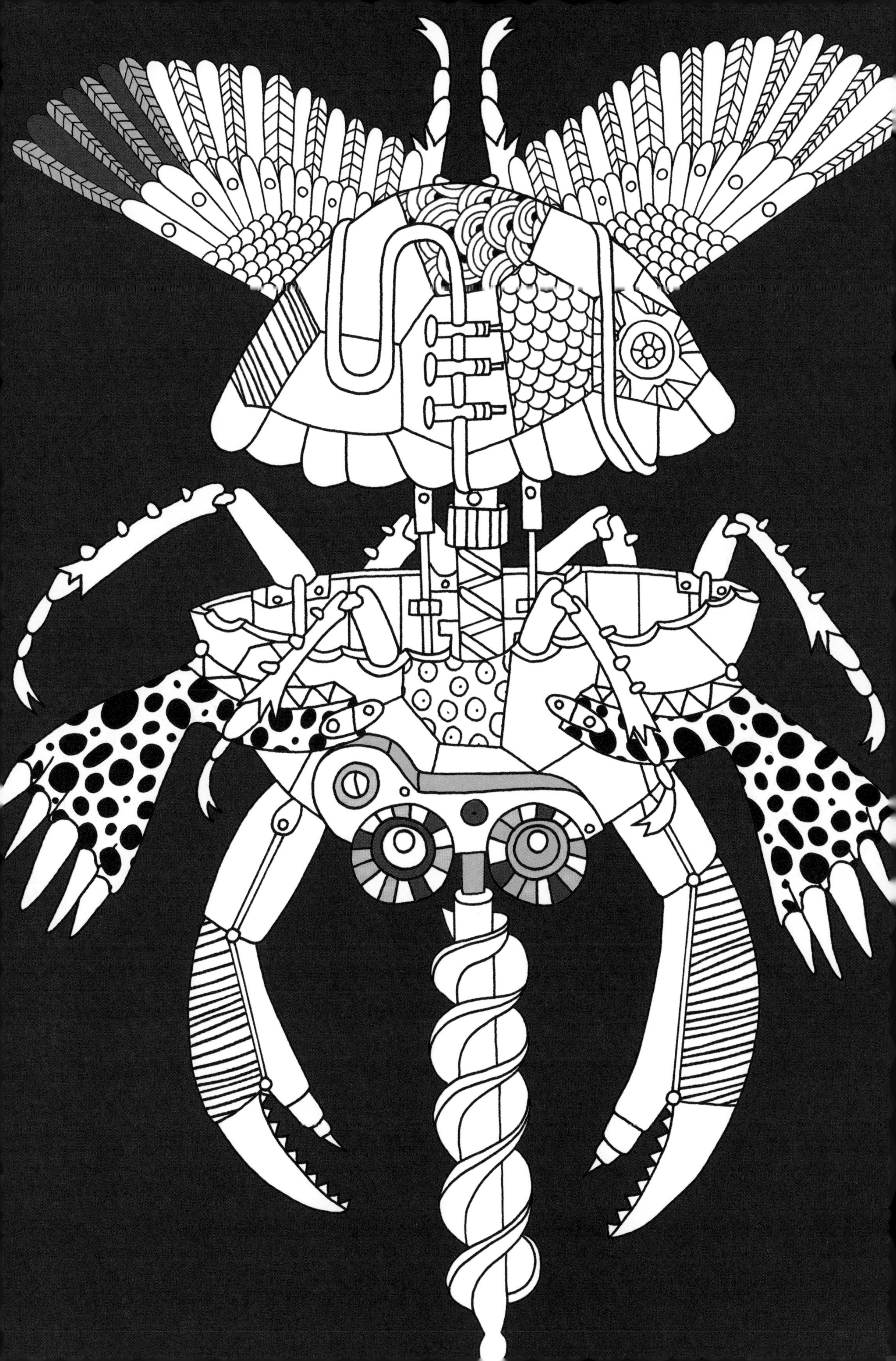

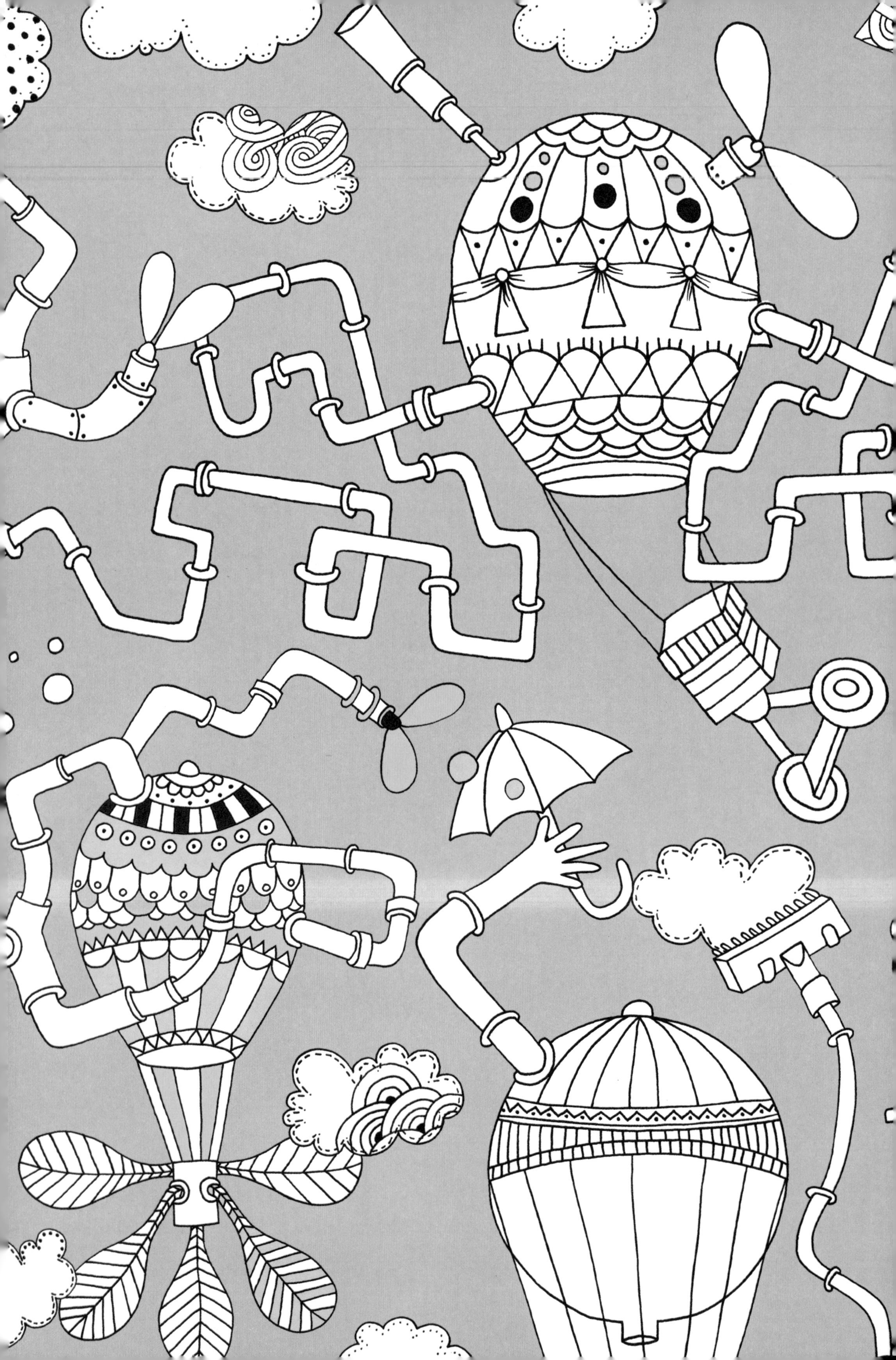

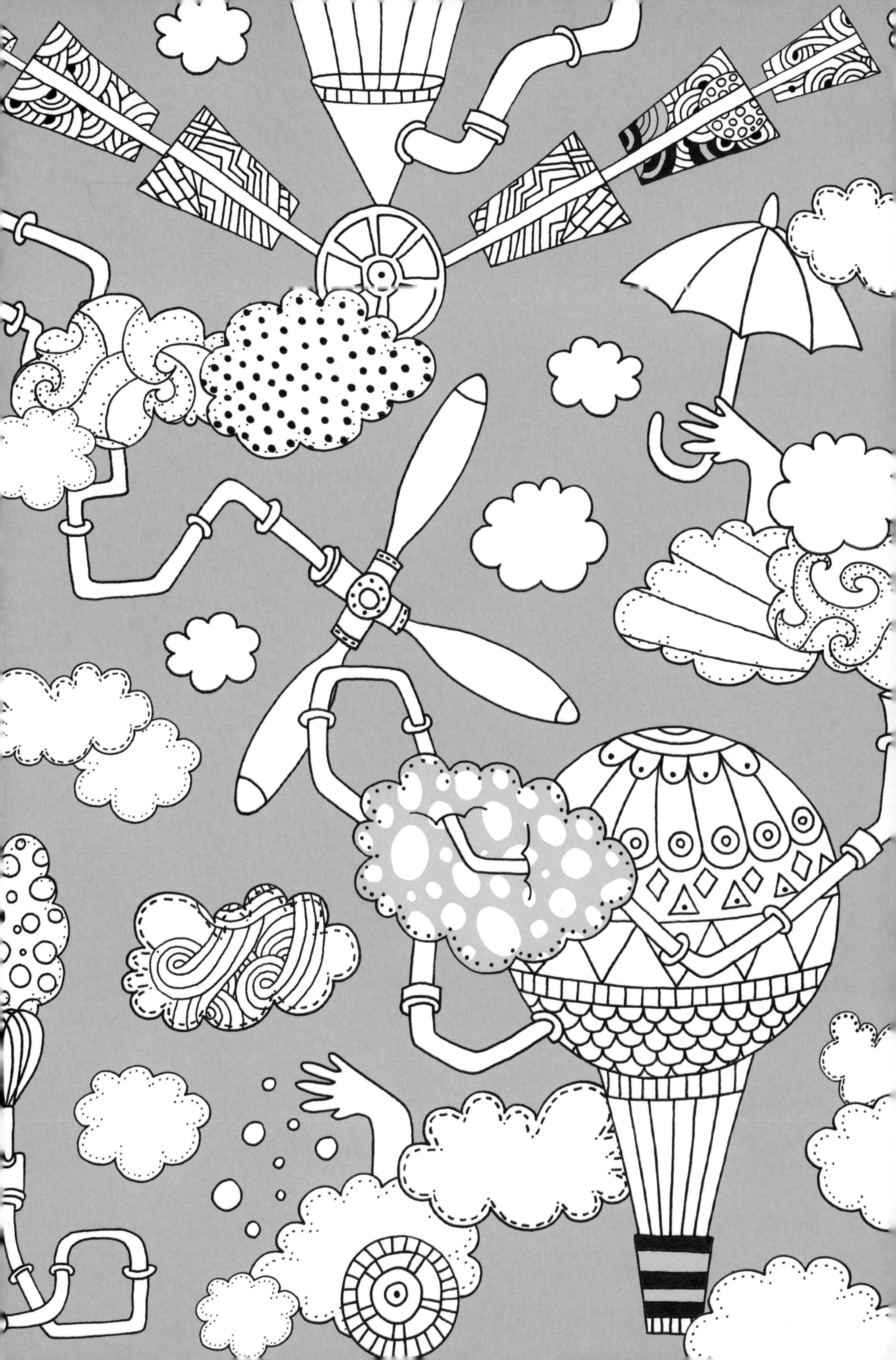

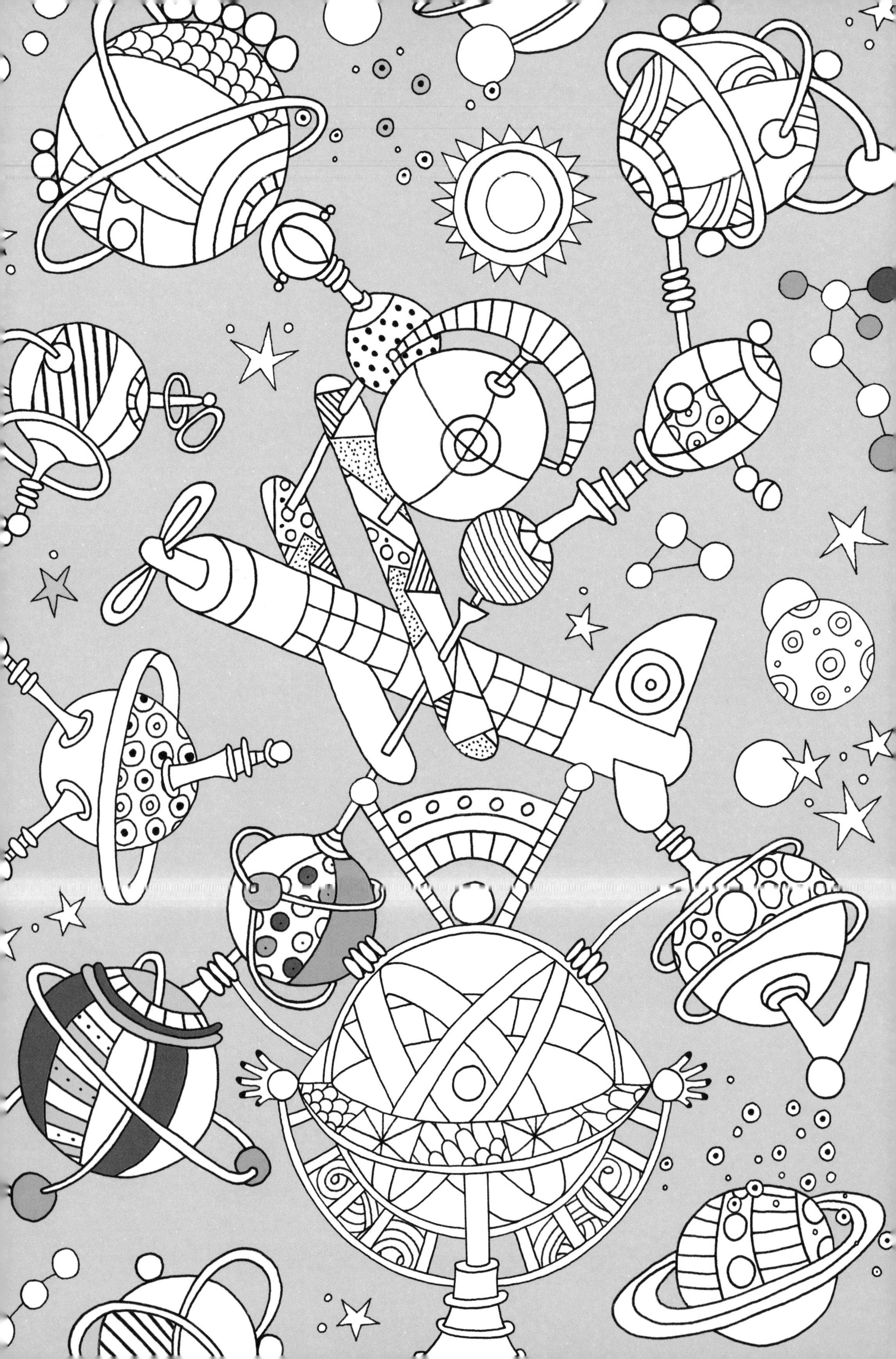

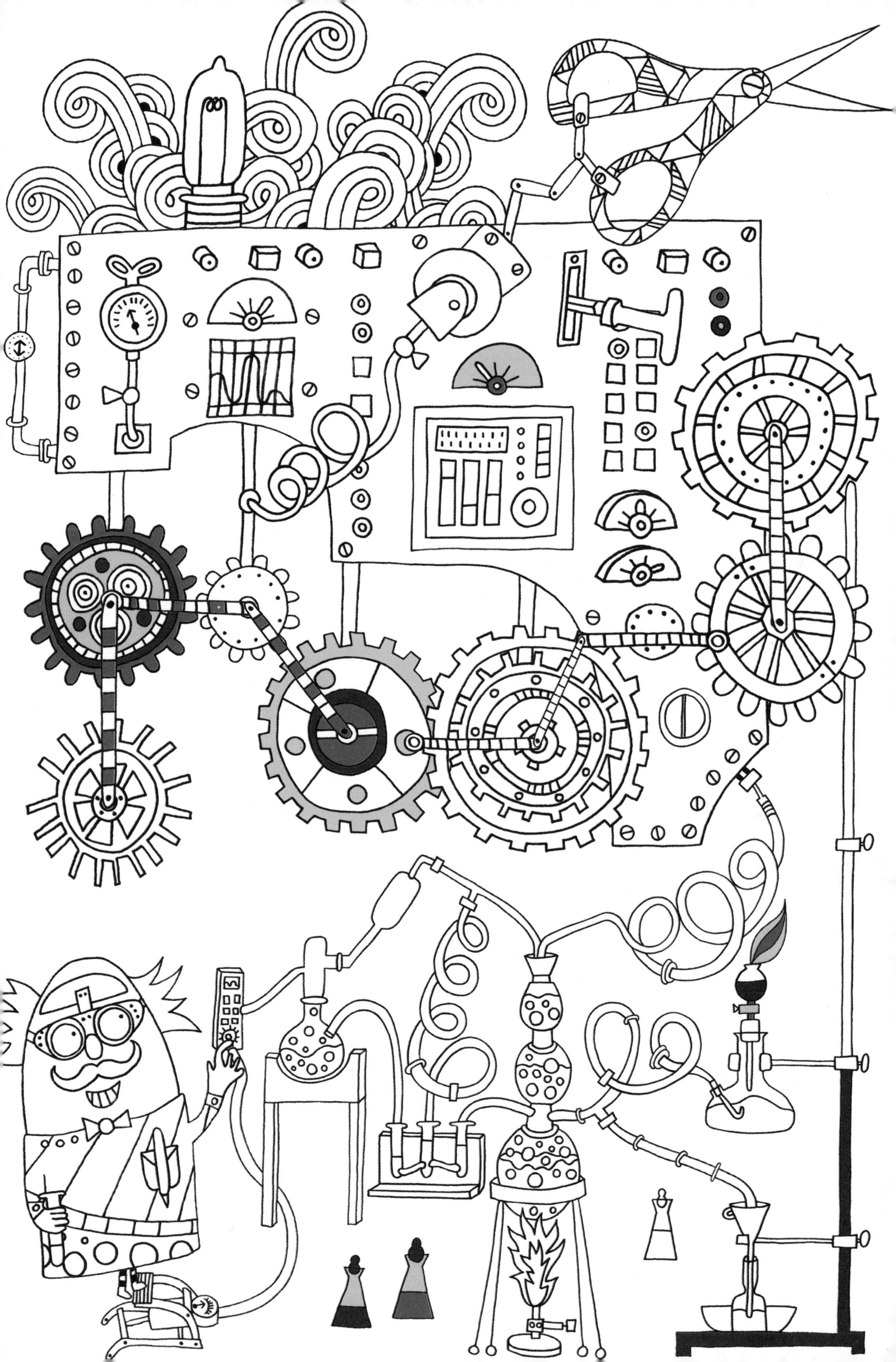

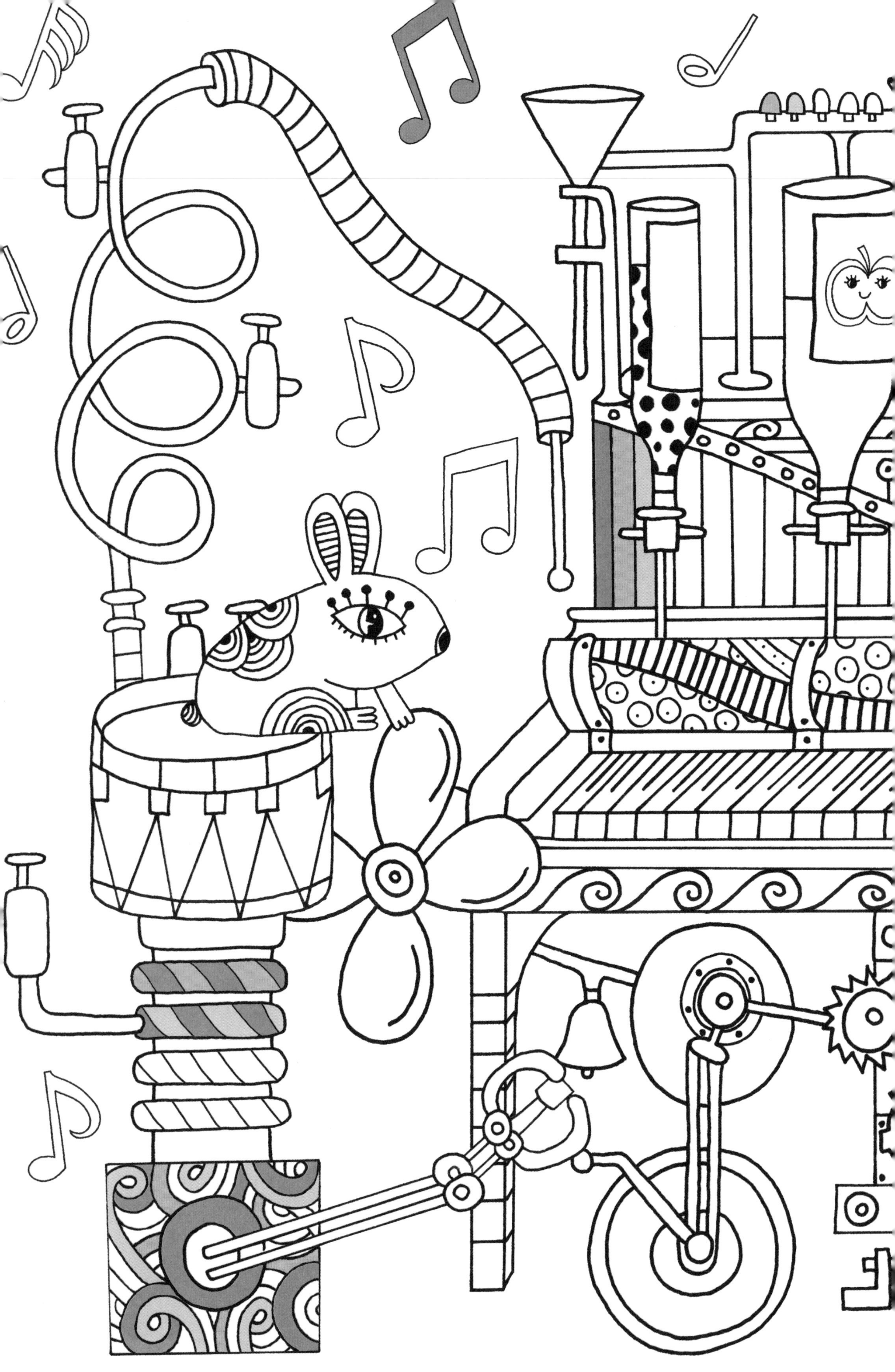

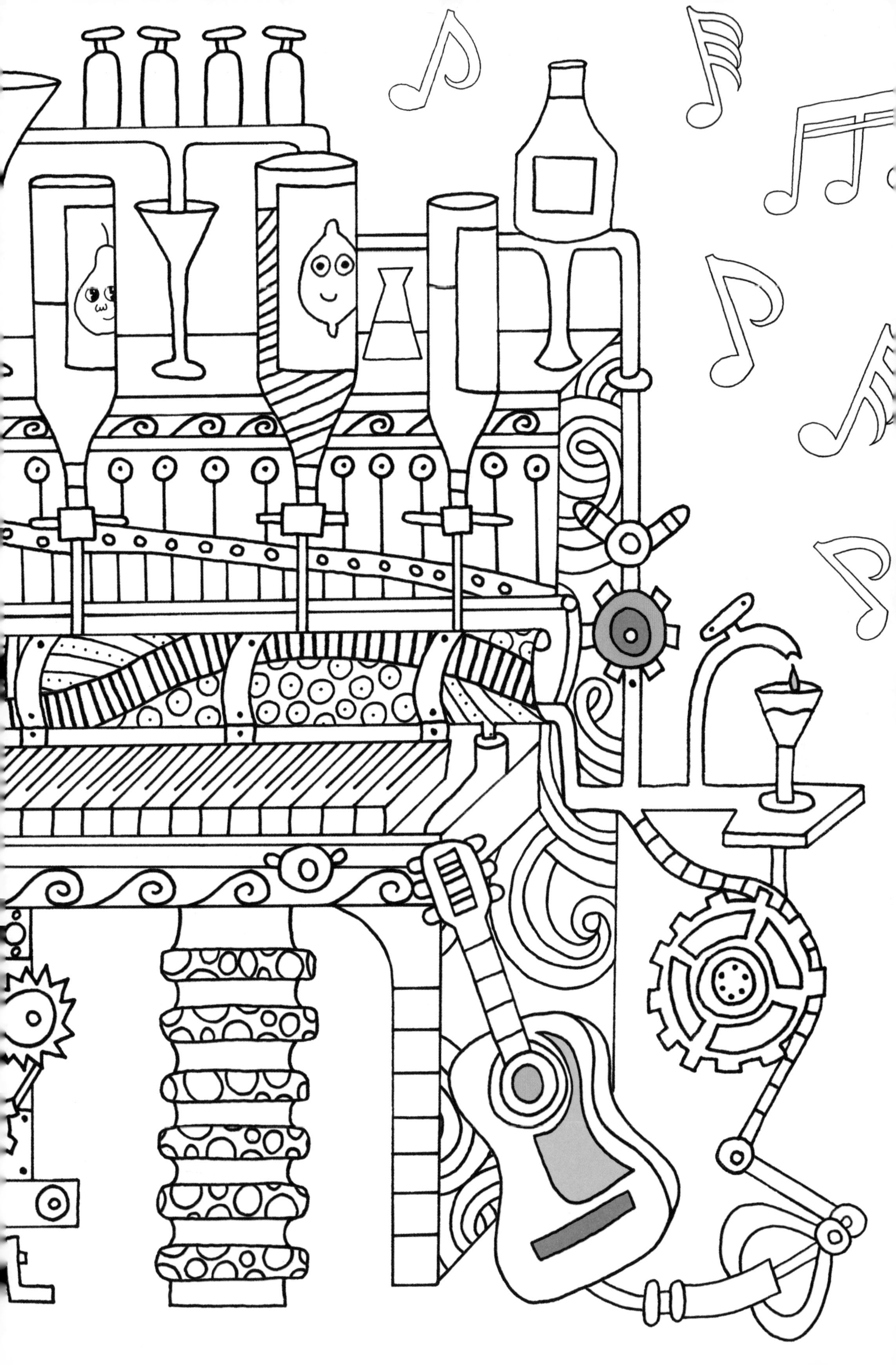

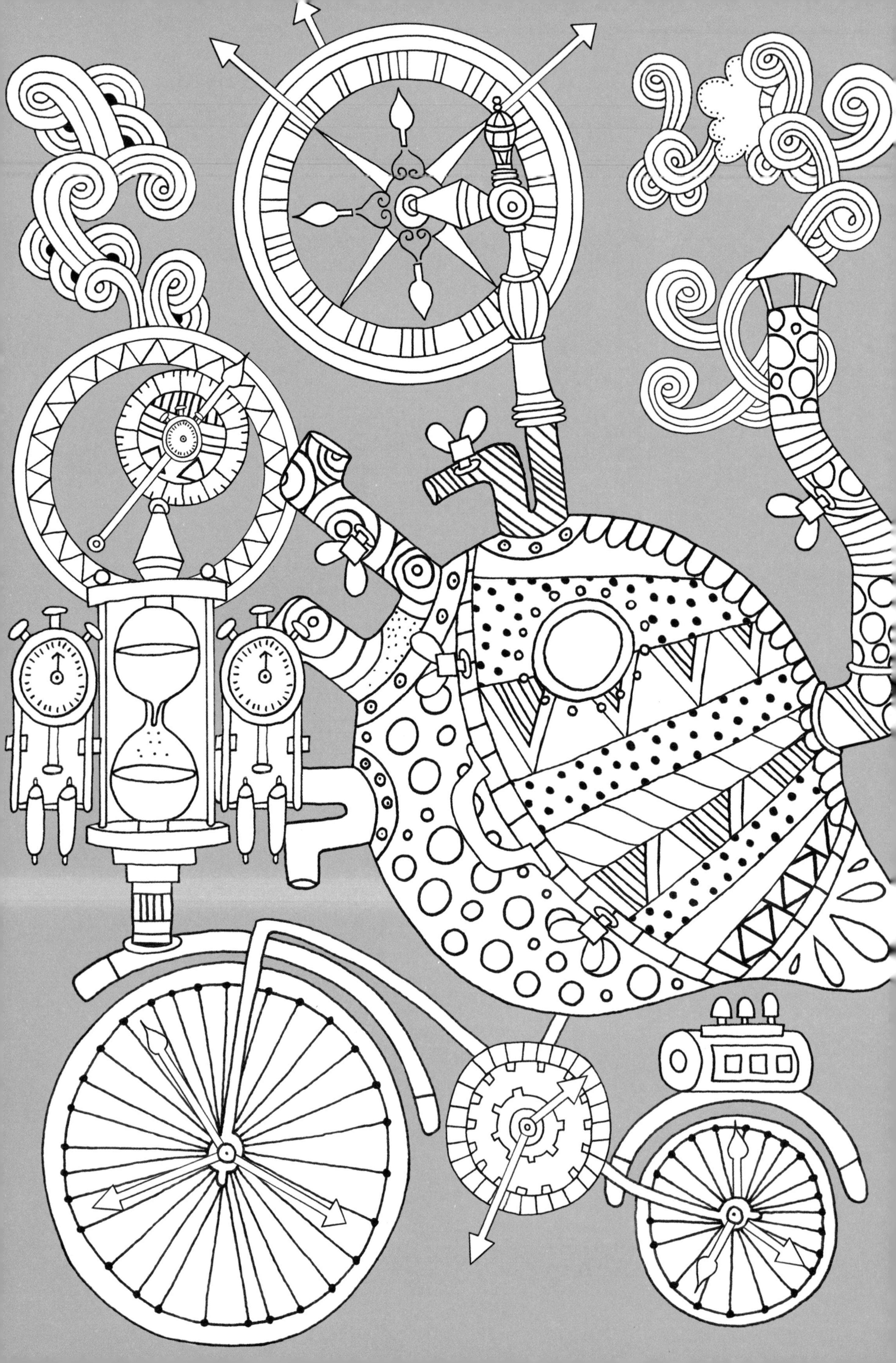

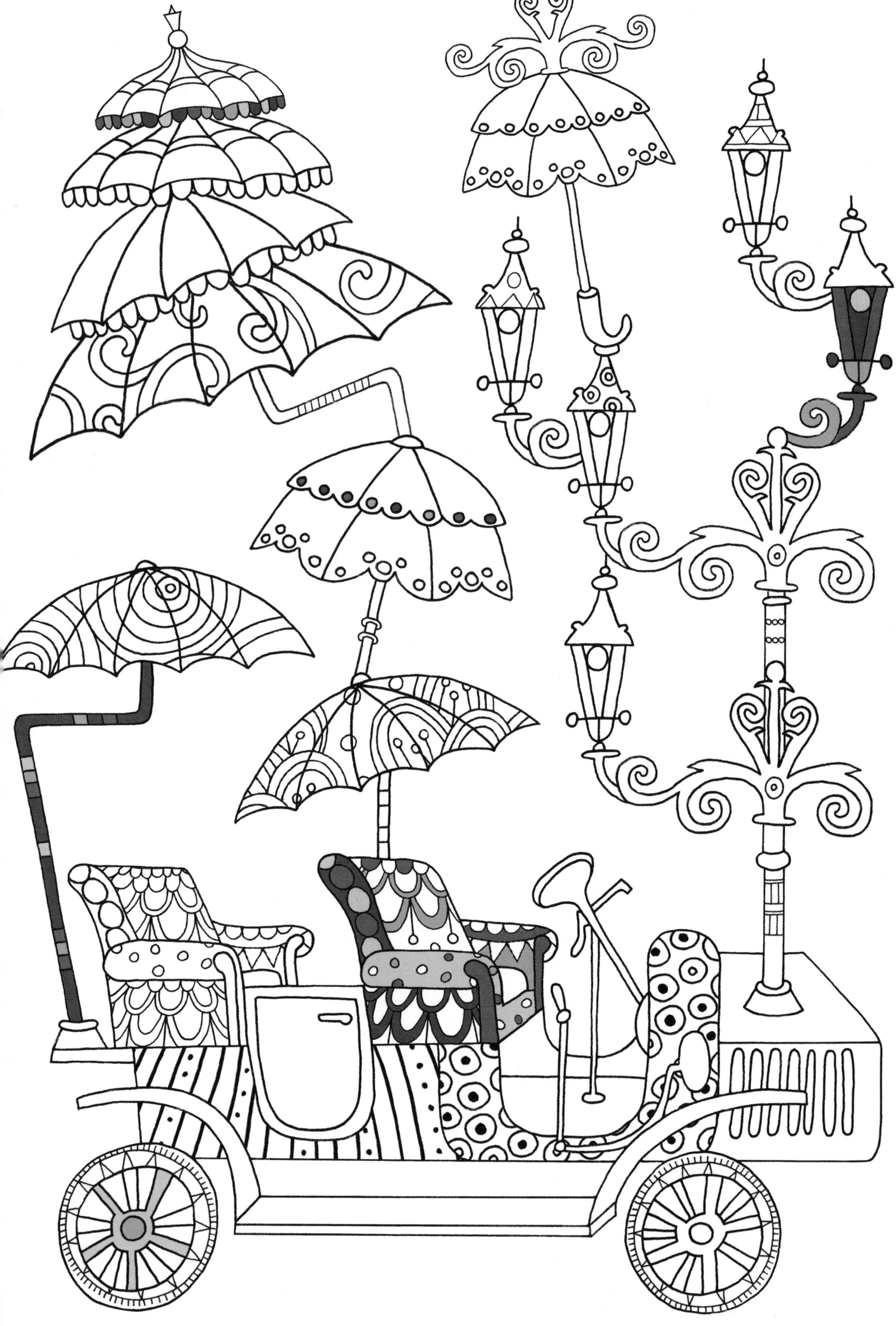

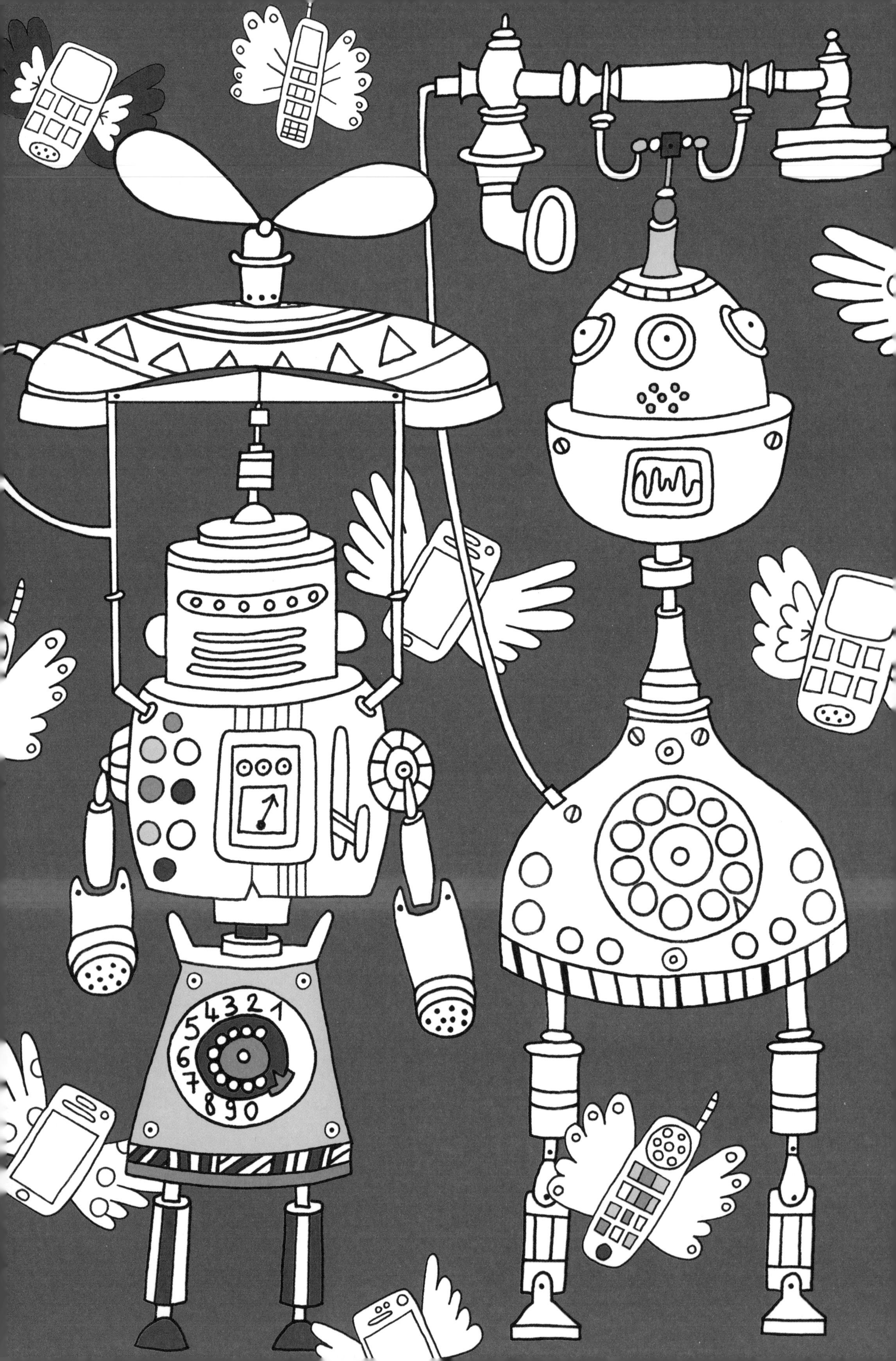
5 4 3 2 1
6
7
8 9 0

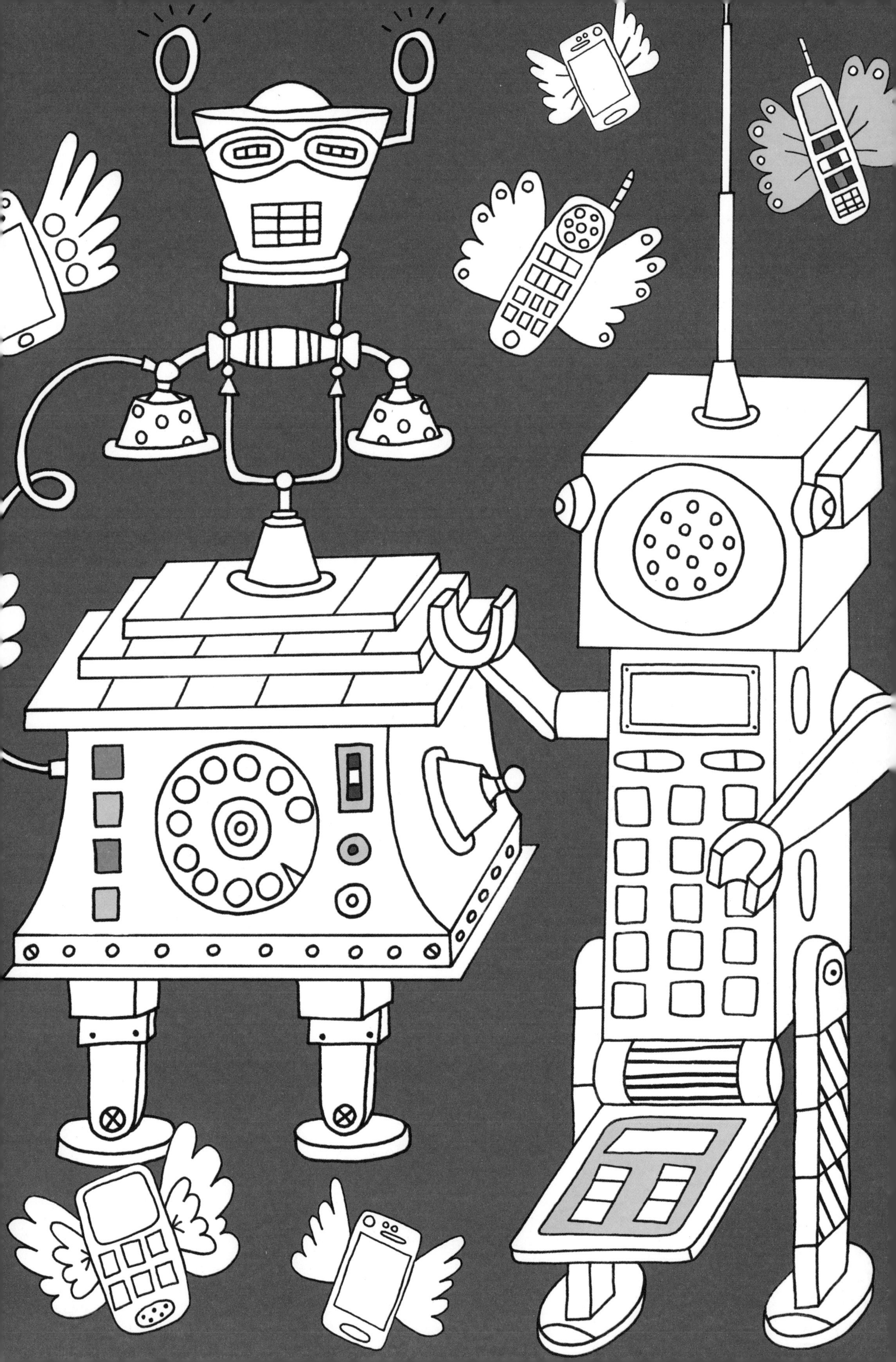

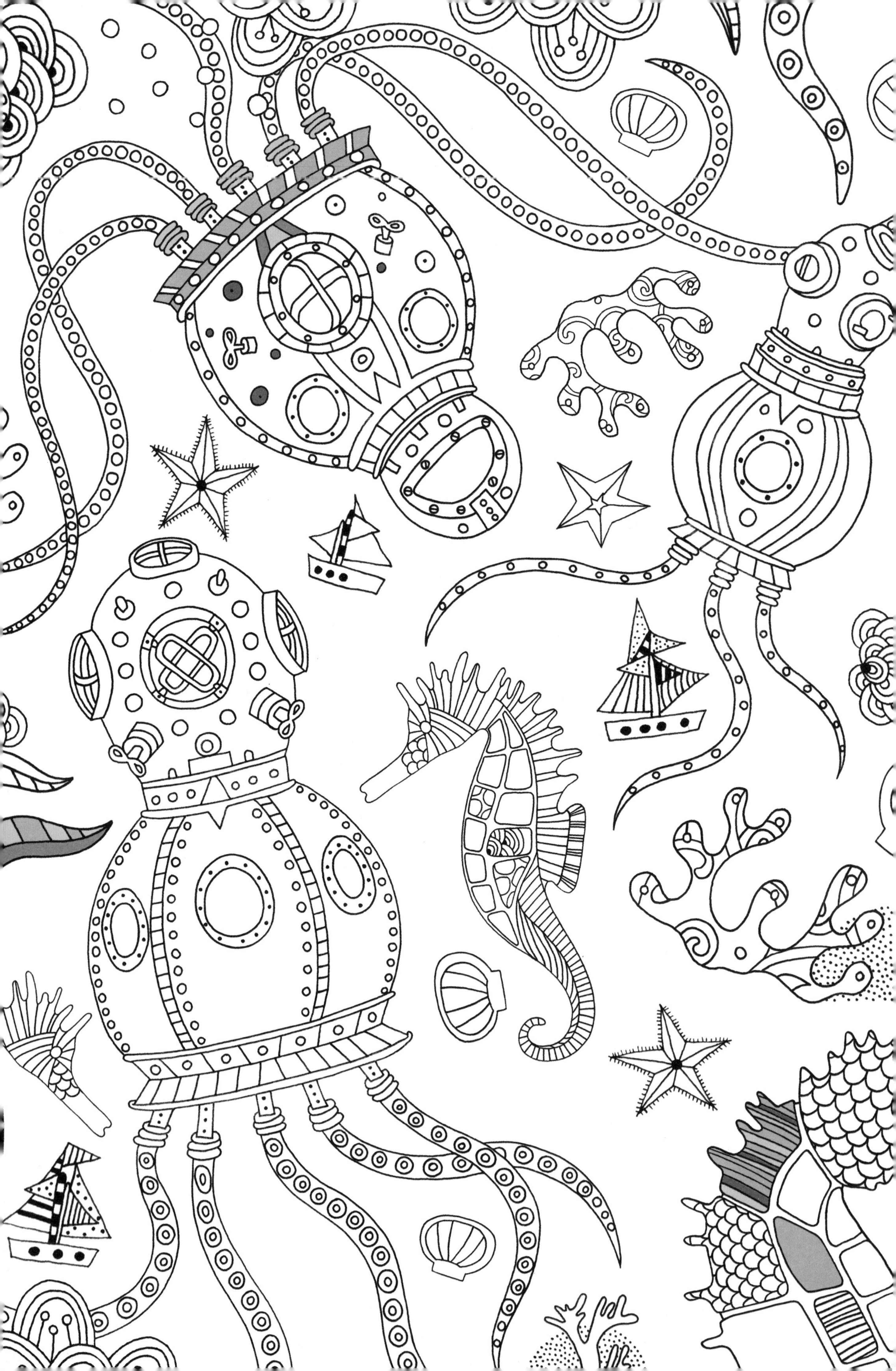

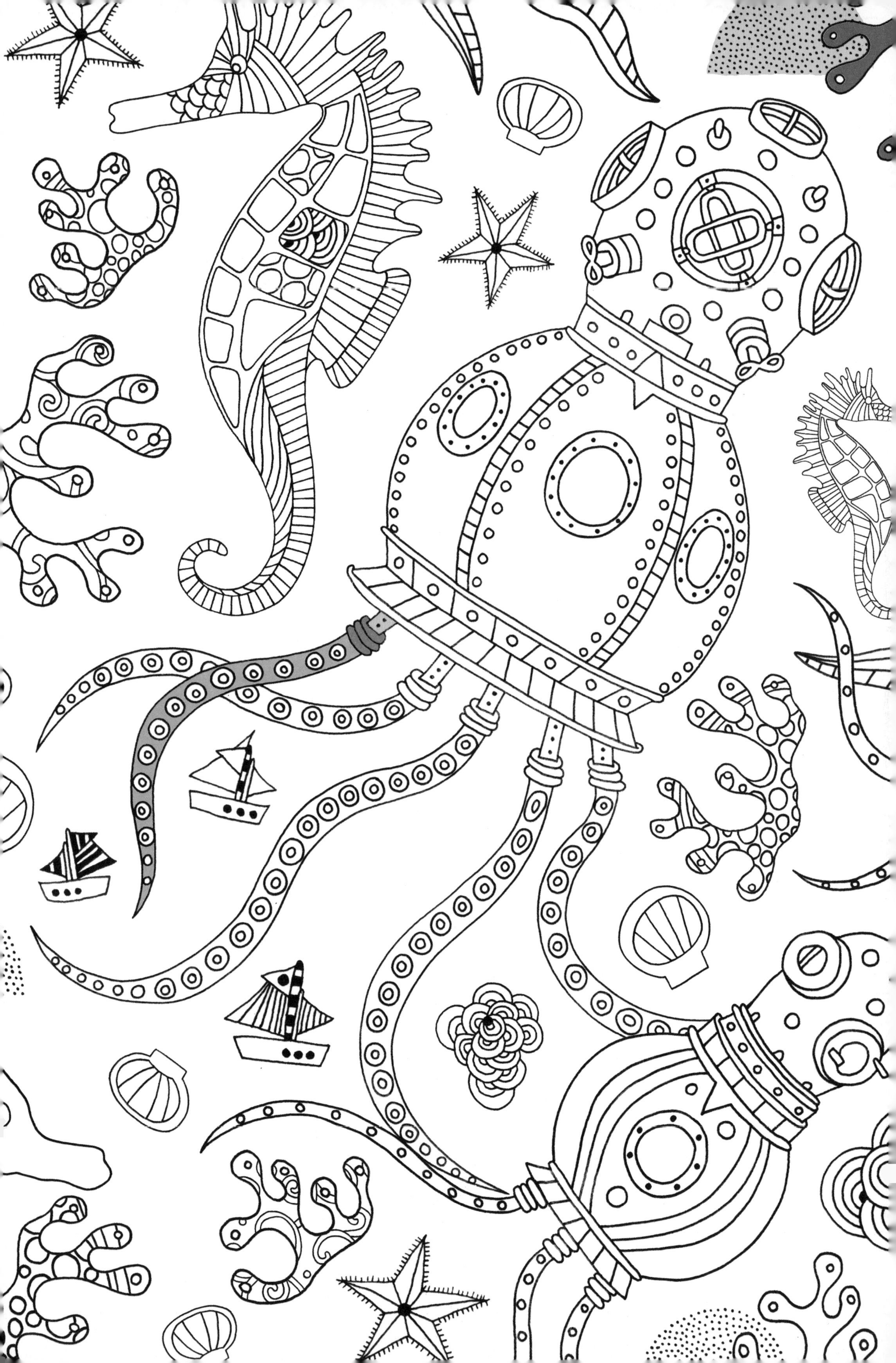

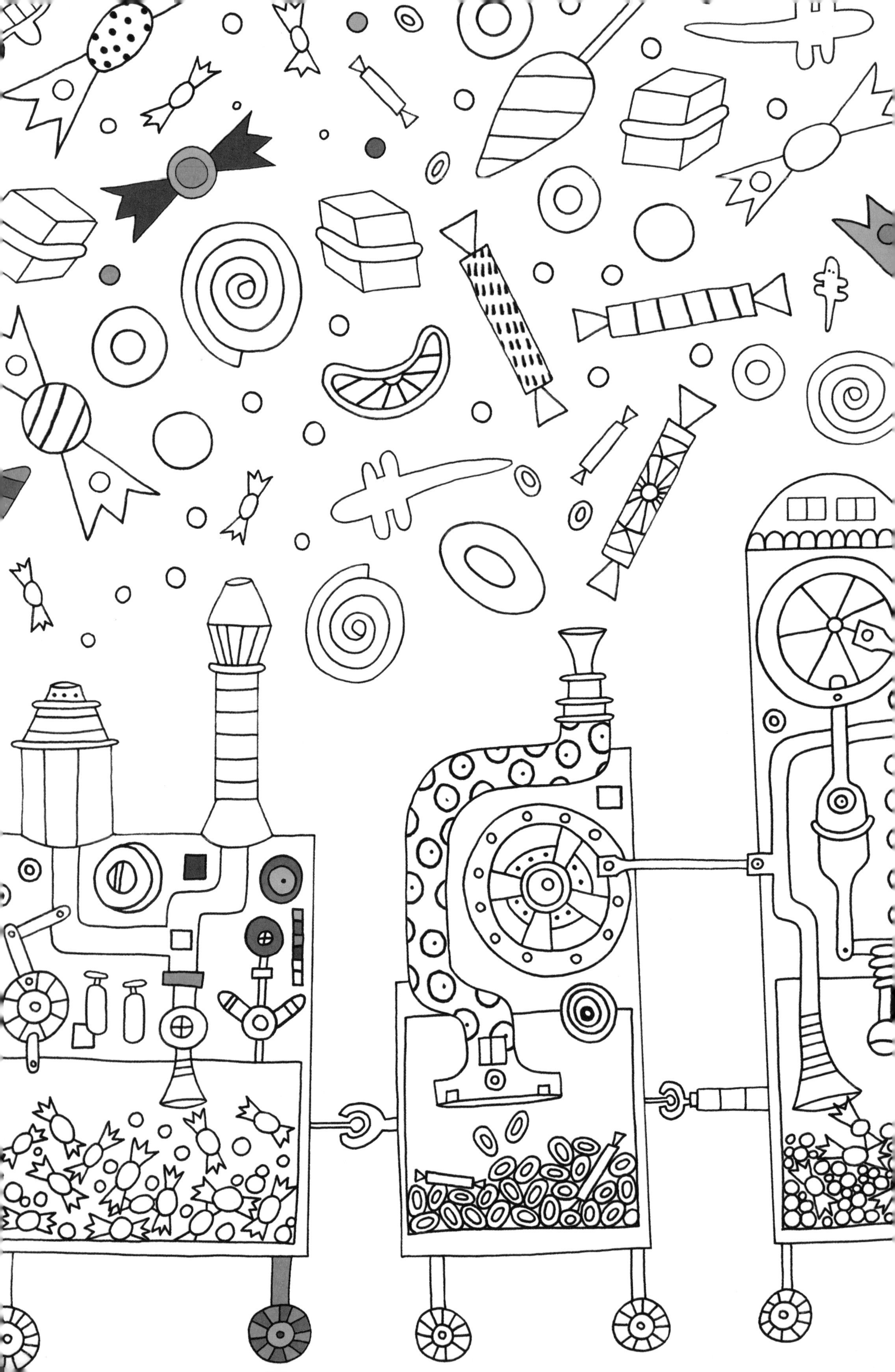

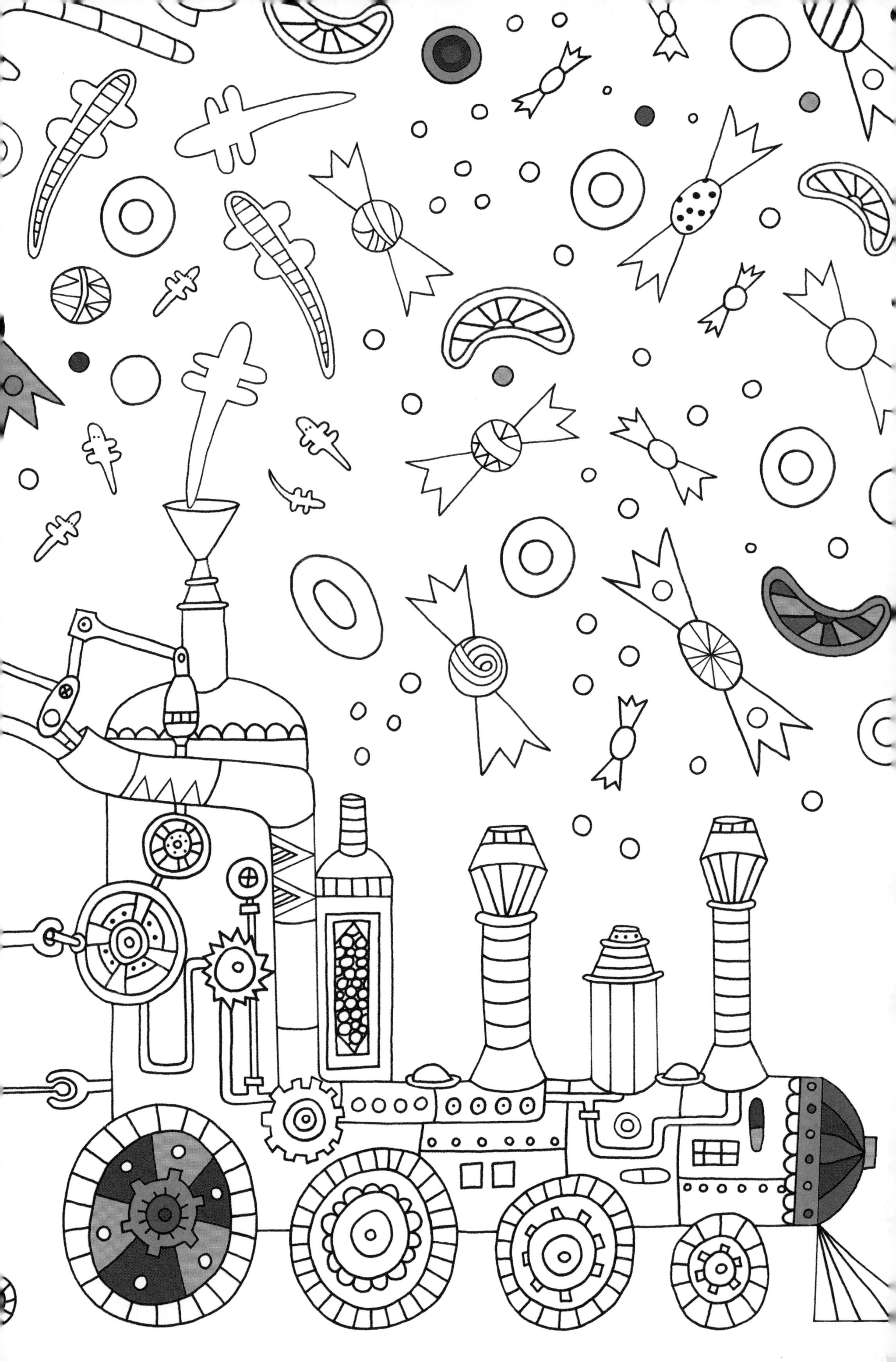

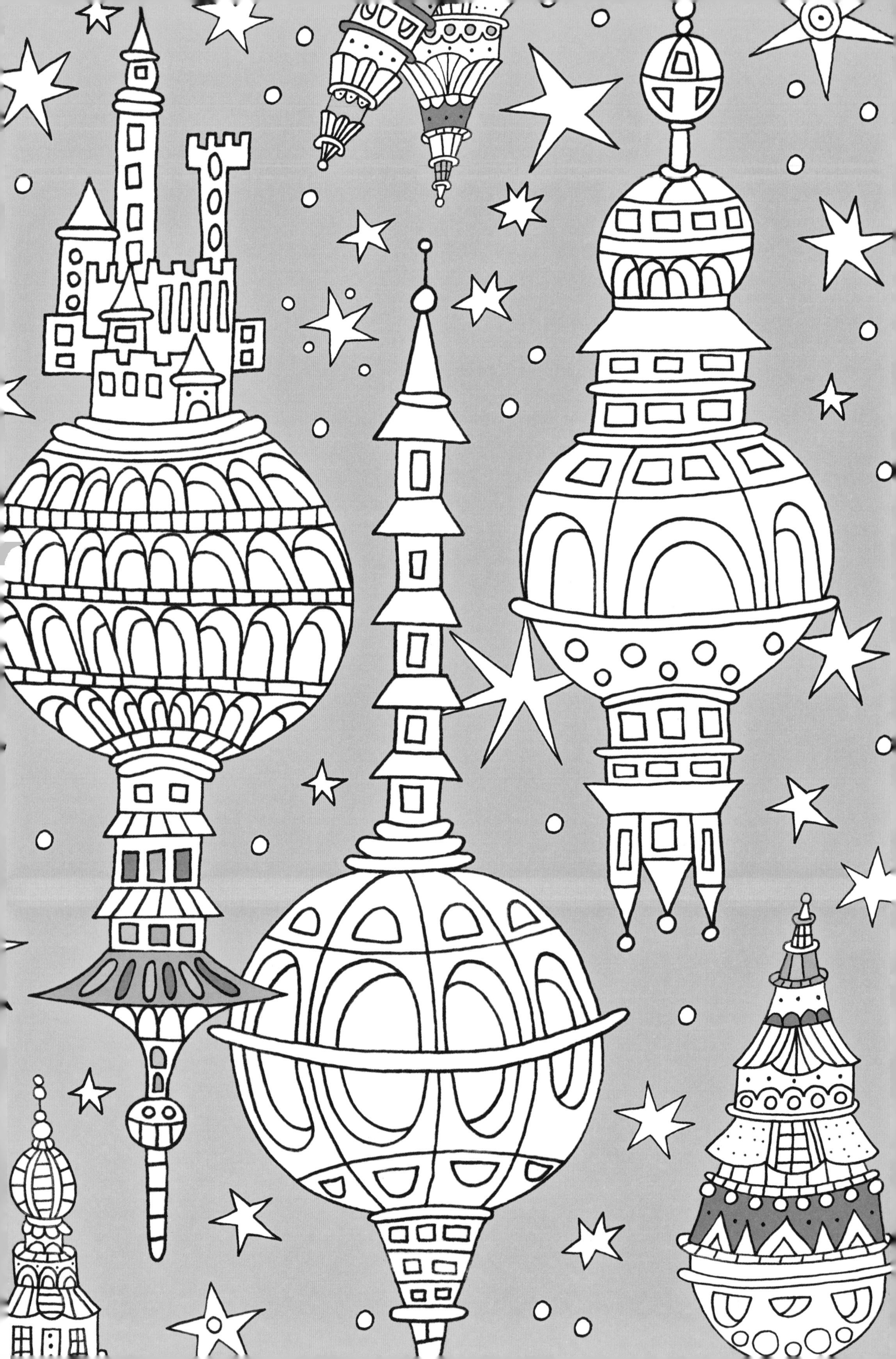

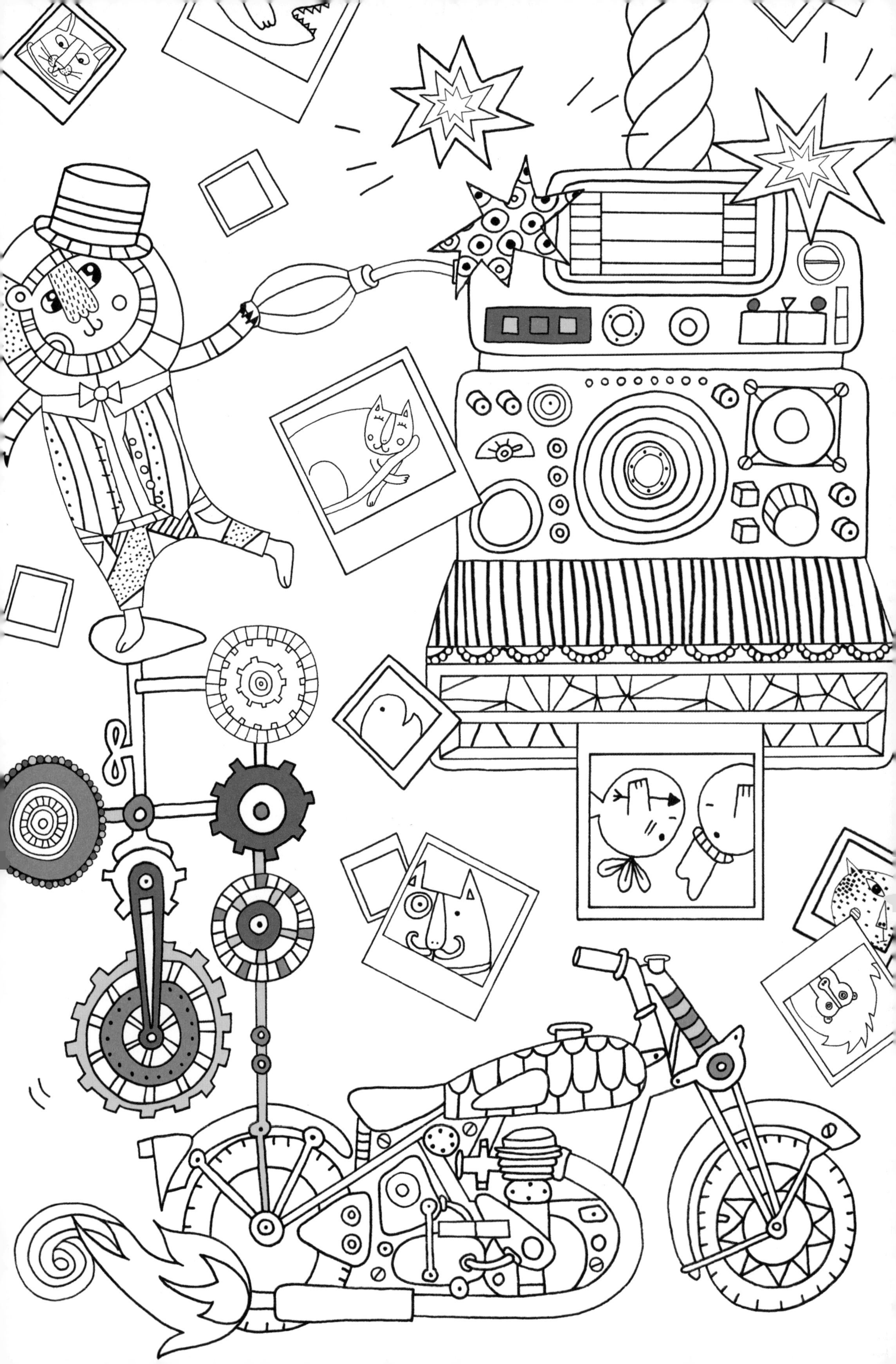

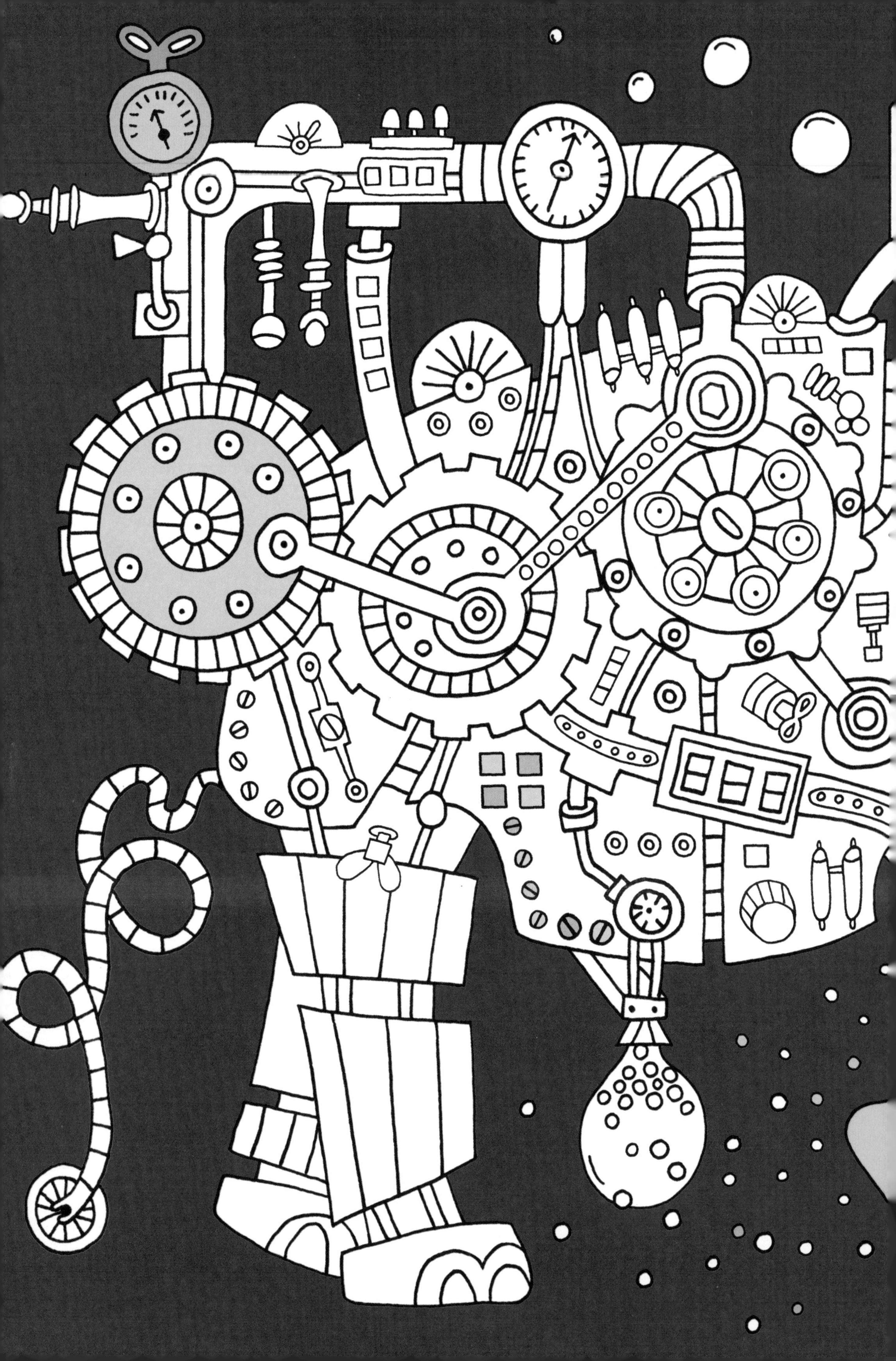

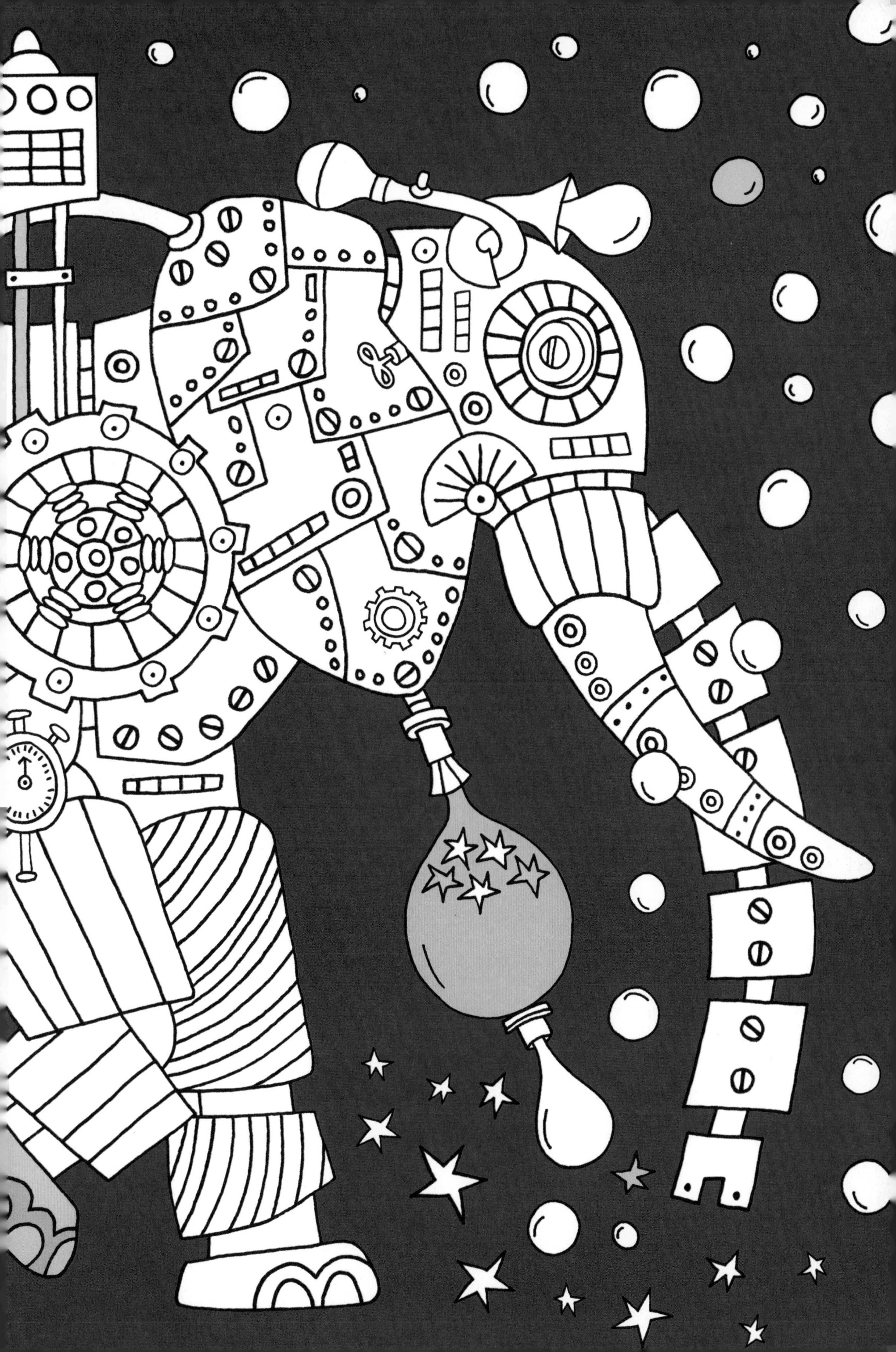